MW01233602

Love Triumphs!

Rescued from the Deep Wounds and
Dark Secrets of Childhood Sexual Abuse

By

Mary Ann Otley

I am convinced that His love will triumph over all life's troubles.
Romans 8:38

Copyright © 2021 by Jesus House of Prayer - All rights reserved.

All rights reserved. No part of this publication may be reproduced or transmitted in any form or by any means electronic or mechanical, including photocopy, recording, or any information storage and retrieval system now known or to be invented, without permission in writing from the publisher, except by a reviewer who wishes to quote brief passages in connection with a review written for inclusion in a magazine, newspaper, website, or broadcast.

Unless otherwise marked, all Scriptures are taken NEW AMERICAN STANDARD BIBLE®. Copyright © 1960, 1962, 1963, 1968, 1971, 1972, 1973, 1975, 1977, 1995 by the Lockman Foundation. Used by permission.

"Love Triumphs"
Lyrics and music by Mary Ann Otley
© 2021 Mary Ann Otley

Published in the United States by Jesus House of Prayer
www.jesushouseofprayer.org

Manufactured in the United States of America 10 9 8 7 6 5 4 3 2 1

Books are available in quantity for promotional or premium use. For information on discounts and terms, please visit our website: www.lovetriumphs.com

Jesus House of Prayer
Cumming, Georgia, USA

This book is dedicated to Jesus!
Your Love triumphs over every storm and transforms my heart.

God is Love, and all who live in love live in God,
and God lives in them.

1 John 4:16

Acknowledgements

First, I would like to thank my husband, Tom. Without you, my story would have had a very different ending, never been written (or completed). Your blessing, love and support are my greatest treasures.

A special thanks to my children, Tommy, Sarah (daughter-in-love), Johnny & Iris. Your lives forever changed mine and brought growth and healing to me in every way. Sarah, your input, and ideas on how to tell my story had breakthrough impact.

An additional thanks to Helen, without your fervent prayers and beautiful example, I don't know where I would be. And Lori, without your unwavering support and intercession, I would not have experienced God's voice through the uncertain times. Angela, thank you for being my cheerleader and encouraging me to finish the race. Gina, you bless my heart.

This book would not have been possible without Elsie. Sent into my life by God, you taught me to hear Jesus and brought me to the only One who could love the pain away. And to Craig Hill, who introduced me to the Ancient Paths.

To Jo, thank you for encouraging me do the right thing, even when it is the hard thing. To John, I appreciate you encouraging me to be transparent and authentic, and coaching me in my writing.

Special thanks to Jon Thurlow. Although we have never met, I have relied on your gentle worship to help me visit the most painful parts of my story.

This work depicts actual events in the life of the author as truthfully as recollection permits and/or can be verified by research. The names of some individuals have been changed to respect their privacy.

Table of Contents

Introduction

From the age of 13 and well into early adulthood, I found myself in circumstances that left me feeling used and dirty due to sexual abuse and rape. I could not understand why these things were happening to me.

The result of being abused impacted how I viewed myself. When I looked in the mirror, I didn't see me, but a loser, a failure, a mistake, and a disappointment. My misguided identity resulted in making poor and unhealthy life decisions. Everyday challenges and stressful situations seemed amplified, and I often felt impossible to cope. As a result, I looked for comfort from people and things that often caused more harm than good. In response, I harbored feelings of intense guilt, shame, fear, anger, resentment, and bitterness. It was a vicious cycle.

I longed for a sense of freedom from negative emotions and behaviors but felt powerless to obtain it. The humiliation of being violated robbed me of dignity, a sense of safety, and the respect I had so freely felt before. And this is why I struggled so intensely. I tried every solution that I knew was available. I sought relief and fulfillment from every source imaginable, yet I kept coming up short and continuously lived with a sense of hopelessness.

Until one night, alone and desperate, realizing I had exhausted every resource I knew, I cried out to the night sky. It was a turning point, and answers, as well as healing, began to come my way in the place I least expected.

If you have been abused, I share my story with you to give you hope and encouragement and share about a love that can radically transform and heal you.

You may know someone who has been abused. In that case, my journey may help you understand how being sexually abused can dramatically impact a person's life and how your love, patience, and prayers can make a difference.

In the following pages, you will read about a path of trauma to triumph. You will see the secure hand that helped me climb out of the mire of dark emotions that bound and blinded me. I found the truth I had been searching for, and I found the freedom I longed for. Now, I have a safe place to go when life gets tough. The unexpected blessing is that the depths of pain I experienced don't rule me anymore but have become a measurement of the compassion and love I can extend to others.

No matter your age or what you have endured, it's not too late to live a life free from the effects of abuse. As you read the following pages, you will discover a love whose power can triumph over every obstacle life has thrown at you. You can be free from the past, be content in the present, and live toward a bright future.

The Trauma

SWEET BEGINNINGS

It was Dad's idea to name me Mary Ann after my mother. Mom felt uncomfortable about it - she thought it might be too vain. They ended up nicknaming me "Mimi," and to this day, my family still calls me that.

We lived in Southern Illinois, across the Mississippi River from St. Louis, Mo. My parents were hard-working, beautiful people. Mom stayed at home and dedicated her life to taking care of us, while Dad worked as a laborer at the steel-mill.

By the time I was five, I had two younger siblings, with one more on the way. The mornings when I woke up early enough, I would get to see Dad before he left for work. He would encourage me to help mom during the day.

"Be a good girl, Mimi," Dad said as he left for work, "Help Mommy today."

"I will, Daddy. I love you," I answered as I followed him to the door.

I loved being my mom's helper and making dad proud when he found out that I helped Mom. Because I was the oldest, helping out with my younger siblings was expected, and I loved it. My brothers and sisters were my world.

Dad's days working in the steel mill left him exhausted. He came home wanting to relax and often didn't have the patience to entertain us. But the moments he did were always the best. He would make us roar with laughter with his slapstick routines. He pretended to run into walls or bump his head on the door. We would scream, "Again! Again! Daddy, do it again!" And he would

11

act like he was walking away just to bump his head into another wall pretending to fall, making us laugh even more.

One cold October night, Dad came in to tuck my sister and me in bed. Our new baby brother was born, and Mom and our little brother had not returned home from the hospital. In Mom's absence, Grandma stayed with us during the day, and Dad relieved her after returning home from finishing a day's work and visiting Mom and our little brother at the hospital. My younger brother, sister, and I were gripped with excitement about meeting our new baby brother.

As Dad planted a kiss on our foreheads and began to walk out of the bedroom, I called out to him, "Daddy!"

"Yes, Mimi?" he asked. "I can't fall asleep. I'm too cold."

He turned around and smiled, "I can fix that," and confidently returned to my bedside. I felt his big, strong hands tuck the blankets all around me. His hands were always so warm and strong. I felt safe and secure. After he sufficiently tucked us in, he asked, "There. Is that better?"

"Yes, Daddy. You're the best daddy I ever had."

He laughed out loud, replying, "Best Dad you *ever* had? I'm the *only* Dad you ever had!" I heard him chuckle as he left my sister's and my room and walked into my brother's room to tuck him in as well.

The next day, Mom returned home with a beautiful baby boy wrapped expertly in an infant blanket. His big brown eyes looked back at my siblings and me as we pleaded for permission to hold him.

I remember the innocence of my youth. As I ran throughout the yard on hot summer days, I remember stopping for a moment to breathe in the sweet smell of honeysuckle. I remember winter days sporting boots, heavy coats, hats, gloves, and mittens to sled down the empty lot across the street. And I remember when I first sensed that something was wrong with my relationship between my dad and me. As a young girl, I couldn't comprehend or logically process Dad's rejection.

STING OF REJECTION

One night after dinner, we settled in the living room while mom finished the dishes. My siblings and I played games on the floor and took turns sitting on Dad's lap while watching Ed Sullivan on TV. Red Skelton was a guest on the Ed Sullivan Show and a favorite comedian of Dad's. Dad was laughing so hard that there were tears in his eyes. I was eight years old.

I climbed onto Dad's lap and immediately met his rejection.

Dad yelled loudly and sternly, "Mimi, get off my lap! Now!"

He had a look of disgust on his face. I was confused and embarrassed. I didn't understand; I just wanted to be close to him. My face felt flushed and burned; tears stung my eyes. Frozen, I looked down in shame. I didn't know what to do with myself. As one of my siblings jumped up on Dad's lap, I winced and prepared myself to hear him yell at them too, but he didn't. Dad kept watching TV as if nothing happened. A sinking feeling came over me. I knew, deep in my heart, that I would never sit there again. *What did I do?* I silently questioned. I felt the first sting of Dad's rejection in my heart.

A sadness came over me that I was too young to express. I didn't realize that I was grieving the physical intimacy and acceptance that I had once freely shared with Dad. I didn't understand that Dad was struggling with something beyond what my young mind could grasp. It felt mountainous, and I carried the mountain-sized disappointment.

Dad's behavior could be erratic and confusing. His fuse was short and often punished us harshly. At the same time, he could be very loving. Like the time I had fallen from my bike while racing down the street and broke my leg. It was a Sunday afternoon. Sundays were "family" days when friends were not allowed to come over, and we were to enjoy family at home. I snuck out of the yard and raced down the street on my bike. A mist had fallen on the hot tar-stained road. The street was slick, and as I sped out of control, I slammed on the brakes and flew into a spin. It was a horrible break, and the doctor suggested that I not be moved around the house until the bone began to heal. Obeying the doctor to keep still, I slept on the couch in the living room the first night in my full-leg cast. The unfamiliar noises of being downstairs alone scared me, and I called out to Dad and Mom. Dad came down, reassured me that I was safe, and put an Andy Williams album on the turntable that sat on a table in the corner of the room to comfort me and drown out any unfamiliar noises.

I felt safe and drifted to sleep listening to Moon River's gentle melodies and Pennies from Heaven. *I love Daddy.*

BE NICE - BE GOOD

Every family has cultural norms and rules for how we are supposed to behave. In my family, there was an expectation of being nice and being good. It was communicated to me at ten years old, in 5th grade. Dad had a system when we brought home our report cards. We would stand in a line in the kitchen while he sat on the couch in the living room. Dad would call us in one by one. We would walk to the living room and sit next to him while he reviewed our grades with us. Being the oldest, I went first and nervously hoped I had good grades and he would be proud of me. As Dad opened my report card, my eyes quickly glanced at the written letters next to each subject. I sighed with relief when I saw an A and some Bs and a C.

"Mimi, we need to get that English grade up from a "C" to a "B.""

"OK, Dad," I replied.

After Dad reviewed my report card that day, he shared his heart with me, "Mimi, it's important that you do well in school, but there is something that is even more important. I want you to be nice to people, and I want you to be a good person. That is what God wants, and that is what I want. I want you to be a nice person and a good person."

Rarely did I hear Dad counsel me, and I could tell this was very important to him. I looked into his beautiful blue eyes and told Dad that I would be nice and try to be good, and he lovingly and approvingly kissed me on the head, "good girl." *Dad's a good person.*

Dad was sincere and genuine when he instructed me to be nice and be good. He told me stories about the good things his dad did to help people in need. Dad was giving me direction, and I appreciated it. I wanted to know what he expected of me, and I wanted to please him. Of all the conversations he had with me, this one was the most influential. The expectation of being nice and good was foundational to my identity. And although it was a positive encouragement on the surface and are character traits I still value today, living to be nice and good without boundaries and guidance when people were not nice and good to me had a destructive impact on my life.

Later that year, my fifth-grade class was returning to our classroom after lunch. Sr. Laurentine was a towering and stern teacher. She meticulously ran her classes with precision and strict discipline. One day I wore a red scarf around my head to school, and she snatched it off my head, called me a witch, and ordered me to stand in the corner. Confused and embarrassed, I stood in the corner until she ordered me to sit at my desk.

Sister Laurentine was ill one day, and a young substitute was teaching in her place. Miss Becker was having a challenging time corralling us while everyone was getting settled in their seats.

Two of my classmates, Mike and Raymond, were in the boys' cloakroom and motioned to me to come in, "Mimi, come you have to see this!"

Curious, I stepped in while Raymond held me down, and Mike placed his hand under my uniform, touching me in places I had never imagined another person would touch. I frantically pulled my way out of Raymond's grip and began to run out of the cloakroom, forgetting about the class full of peers. Rattled and embarrassed, I quickly found my way to my desk while Mike and Raymond walked out of the cloakroom with big smiles on their faces. *Why would they do that!? What's going on? Does everyone else know what they did? Will they tell my parents? This would have never happened if Sr. Laurentine was here. Will Sr. Laurentine find out? What will she do to us? Why did they pick me?* Confused, I struggled to know how to respond to what had just happened. *Be nice, Mimi, be good. Be nice, be good.* Miss Becker began teaching us, and I hoped my classmates would never find out. I avoided Mike and Raymond for years until the eighth grade.

On the first day of eighth grade, I stepped into the classroom and found notebooks placed on each desk. The teacher instructed us to find the desk with the notebook that had our names written on it. I found my name and sat at my desk. My heart sunk when I saw the name written on the notebook behind me. Raymond White. *Oh no! And we are sitting in the back of the classroom! What else is he going to do to me?* My heart raced. As I sat at my desk, I heard Raymond settle at his, and dread came over me when I felt Raymond tap me on the shoulder.

His touch disgusted me. "Mimi," he whispered.

"What?" I responded without turning back to look at him.

16

"I'm sorry about what happened," he whispered.

Tears stung my eyes as I recalled Raymond holding me down while Mike touched me. Relief flooded my heart, and I turned around and whispered, "It's OK."

"It was wrong. I felt a lot of pressure to do it. I shouldn't have," Raymond explained. Raymond and I became good friends after that moment until we graduated and moved on to different high schools. I hid that moment in my heart and treasured it because I thought it was a very courageous thing for him to do. I admired him for it.

Later that year, I complained to my mom about a toothache. She made an appointment and drove me to the dentist with younger siblings in tow. Mom and my siblings remained in the waiting room while I followed the hygienist into a room, instructing me to sit in the dentist's chair. She placed a bib on me and let me know that the dentist would be right in to take care of my cavity. I heard dentist enter the room, and it sounded as if he locked the door. *He must not want to be interrupted so he can do a good job on my tooth.*

Mom had explained that the dentist would need to use a drill to remove the cavity. He never spoke to me. I remember that as he drilled my tooth, I could feel the pressure of the drill and the strength of his hands in my mouth. I was intimidated by him, and then a terrifying and unexpected thing began to happen. While I was sitting in his chair waiting for the filling to cure, he began to touch parts of my body. He fondled my small breasts, and intense fear gripped me. *What is going on? Why is he touching me this way? What is happening?*

I was terrified and confused. I was confused mostly that my body responded to his touch. The feelings were powerful and frightened me. My body had never experienced the feelings I was

17

feeling. I wanted to run but didn't know how. *Be nice, be good. Be nice, be good.*

I couldn't think of how to be nice and to be good at that moment. I froze and clenched my eyes closed until he was done. The last thing I can remember of that dentist visit is never wanting to see him again. I was terrified and had shut down. I don't remember walking out of the office or anyone taking me to my mom. I just remember the shame and guilt and fear I experienced and the powerlessness I felt. I don't know how and don't ever remember making a conscious decision to do so, but I shoved the memory, the shame, the guilt, and the fear deep down somewhere within my being. I didn't remember what happened until I was in my 30s.

When I shared it with my mother, she was heartbroken and recalled that she could not make me go back to the dentist. I wouldn't budge. At the age of 13, I was adamant about seeing my best friend's dentist instead.

FALLING APART AT THE SEAMS

Over time, it was apparent that Dad and Mom's life had become increasingly difficult. Dad looked tired and drained. He was impatient with himself, and he was impatient with us. His expectation of me being nice became "making no waves or conflict," and me being good meant "don't do anything that would cause embarrassment." As life became more and more stressed, I understood that I was never to question authority, talkback, or stick up for myself. These offenses would be met with disapproval and punishment.

At home, behind the scenes, turmoil was brewing. Dad drank often. There were nights when he didn't come home for dinner. One night I suspected he didn't come home at all because we were out of diapers, and Mom said she would get them and groceries when Daddy came home from work. The next morning, Dad was not home, and we still needed groceries and diapers.

Dad and Mom's relationship was deteriorating. I noticed the sadness in Dad's beautiful, blue eyes and frustration in my lovely mother's voice. I began writing poems to them about love to convince them to love each other again. Mom would hug me, and Dad would thank me, but discontent had taken root. My poems and effort to get them to love each other were futile. The flame in their relationship had ceased to burn. They hid it well for many years, but things were now quickly spiraling out of control. They mostly argued and fought privately. But Dad expressed his frustration one night by yelling at Mom and throwing a piece of chicken across the dining room table at her because Mom had burnt it. Fearful and in disbelief, it was becoming clear that our happy family was falling apart.

As my family was unraveling, it was also increasing. My baby sisters were born two years apart, making us a family of six children. My sisters added so much fun and love to my life. My favorite memories are holding them as infants, watching them learn to walk, and taking them for walks in our neighborhood. Their innocence, sweet voices, and fun antics were a joy amidst increasing chaos.

Finances had become a source of contention between Dad and Mom. Mom had started working at a local hospital to earn more money, and babysitters filled her space until Dad came home from work. The transition from having mom at home caring for us to her leaving for work was difficult. She had always been home base, an anchor, which felt very foreign, and I felt uncertain and fearful about what was happening to our family.

Our family sold our home and moved in with Grandma, Dad's mother. To my siblings and me, it was the equivalent of moving to Disney World. Being with grandma meant unlimited pizza, decorating cupcakes, and doing whatever you wanted to do. She hosted the best sleepovers ever!

I was very excited when we moved in with grandma, and I remember reflecting, "This will be good. Maybe things will work out. Grandma knows how to 'handle' Dad." He was never cross around her.

My siblings and I celebrated moving to Grandma's with cheers of excitement, but to Dad and Mom moving out of their own home and into Grandma's was an act of desperation and a symbol of failure.

I thought moving to Grandma's would give us help, a new beginning, a way to recover. But things got worse, much worse.

SILENT TEARS

I was 13 years old when babysitting opportunities became a steady way to earn cash. It was past midnight, the house was dark, and everyone was asleep when I came home from babysitting our next-door neighbor's ten-month-old girl. Typically my pajamas were two pieces that included a top and shorts. But that night, it was hot in the room, and I slipped on a hand-me-down, red and white striped nightgown my aunt had given me. It fell at knee level. It still smelled just like her, and that was comforting as I slipped into bed and drifted off.

Waking up out of a deep sleep, my heart knew I was in danger before my brain did because my heart was beating like a drum before my brain could discern why. Something frightening was happening. Someone was touching me in an unfamiliar and uncomfortable way. A man was in my bed lying next to me. Still under the covers, my pajamas had slipped up, and my backend was exposed, and he was touching me in private places. Terror-stricken; a sick feeling came over me. I kept my eyes closed. I didn't want him to think I was awake because I was terrified to face him, and I wanted to buy some time. My mind ran a million miles a second, trying to understand what was going on. I immediately reasoned that I had not locked the back door. *How many times did they warn me to lock the back door when I came home at night? This is all my fault! Now this person entered our house and is going to do only God knows what to us. And what am I going to do?* Thinking, thinking, thinking. *If I yell, what will he do? Has he hurt anyone in my family? Am I first or last? What about my brothers and sisters?* The thought of their safety put me in survival mode. *I have to do something. But what do I do? Does he have a knife? Does he have a gun? I can't just lay here.* Then something obvious occurred to me when I noticed the scariest reality of all. Dread filled my mind and heart when I recognized the man's scent. The man smelled familiar. Terror filled my heart as I was forced to accept the truth. The man wasn't a burglar or a mass murderer. He didn't break-in. He lived here—The man was Dad!

It was so incongruent. So confusing. So un-like Dad. *Dad would never do this.* I didn't understand. *What is he doing? Why is he doing this? This is so wrong! This is so bad! What do I do?* It felt so dark. So intimidating. Another thought came to me; I *can't let him know that I know. How will I ever face him? If I yell, what will happen? What will happen to me? What will happen to him? Will I be in trouble? Will he be in trouble? Who do I tell? How do I stop him?* I had an immediate plan. I would pretend I would arouse from sleep. Surely if he saw me wake up, he would leave. He would never do this to me if he thought I was awake. I began to move and pretend I was slowly arousing from sleep, and he didn't stop. *No. No. No. Now I'm in big trouble!* He was so close that I was afraid he could hear my thoughts. Fear gripped me. Surely, he could feel my heart beating. I wished I could scream, *Why Dad? What are you doing?* But I knew better than to confront him. Another instantaneous thought came, *pretend you are having a nightmare.* And without delay, I began screaming frantically with my eyes closed, acting as if I was having the nightmare of nightmares.

The room I slept in was a sitting room. It had two doors, one led to the back of the house toward the kitchen and the other to the front toward the hallway. Dad jumped out of the bed and darted through the back door that led to the kitchen, while Grandma came rushing to investigate through the door that led to the hallway.

She had heard my screams from her bedroom. "Mimi, what's wrong? Are you OK?"

Before I could answer, Dad had quickly walked through the house and followed Grandma into the room, acting just as concerned as she was. "Go back to bed, Mom," he said. "I'll take care of Mimi. I'm sure it was just a nightmare."

My heart was turned inside out. I had never thought of my dad as my enemy, never, not until that night, and the disappointment weighed so heavy on my heart.

I clutched my pillow as Grandma left the room. Dad bent over and looked at me. I looked down in shame.

He said firmly, "It was a nightmare, Mimi, now go back to sleep. You just had a nightmare."

I knew he was waiting for my response, and I whispered, "Yes, Dad. It was just a nightmare," then he walked out of the room.

I put my back to the headboard. From that night on, and well into adulthood, whenever I was sleeping alone in a room, I would sleep with my back against the headboard, so no one would ever approach me from behind again. I tried to stay awake to stand guard, but I fell asleep after who knows how long. But just before I drifted, I heard a voice. It was more like a whisper but with a very authoritative tone. I was sure it was God because it spoke with such certainty, and who else could have known what had just happened.

The voice declared darkly, "You must really be bad for something like this to happen to you."

Shame covered my mind and my heart like a blanket, and I answered, "I must. I must really be bad. This must be my fault."

At thirteen years old, my identity was established, not by a loving, affirming voice, but a condemning, shaming voice. I was a bad girl, and I would never be the same.

The loss of my relationship with dad was another layer of trauma. I didn't realize at the time that it triggered a grieving process. What felt safe and secure was no more. Sexual abuse is so much more than an instance or an experience. For me, it included the death of an important relationship and the loss of feeling protected.

THE TWILIGHT ZONE

Although I felt the weight, I was too young to understand the complexity of what had happened. Again, it was just so incongruent. The man who was supposed to protect me, provide for me, direct me, guide me, affirm me and love me, now terrified me. It was more than I knew how to handle. I had to deal with the aftermath of the events of that night. I lost my dad. Trust was shattered. It felt like someone pushed a button, and the floor came out from beneath me. I was confused, afraid, and carried the shame that, somehow, I was responsible for the incident.

The next morning, I woke up to sounds in the kitchen. My siblings were sitting at the table eating cereal, while Grandma and Mom whispered in the hallway. *Were they talking about me?* I wondered. I heard Grandma mention the word nightmare, and my heart sunk. *Yes, they are talking about me.* I felt like I entered the Twilight Zone. I couldn't shake this bizarre, overwhelming, yucky feeling. I watched my brothers and sisters laugh and tease each other at the kitchen table and felt outside of their world for the first time. While everyday daily life was going on the same, I felt outside of it. I felt separate from my own family and knew it would never be the same. I had a fear that they would not love me anymore. It's the first time I felt unlovable. *How could anyone ever love me? I will never tell them, or they will all be disgusted with me.* My heart hurt. As I looked at my brother and sister from across the room, I vowed, *I'll make them love me. I'll do whatever it takes so they will love me.* From that time on, I believed that love was something I would have to earn because I did not deserve it.

Once I got my composure and entered the kitchen, I asked them, "Where's Dad?"

"I don't know," my brother shrugged.

"He left," my sister replied.

I was relieved that Dad was not home, yet wondered *how will I ever face him?* I walked into the living room and found cartoons playing on the TV. One of the cartoon characters fell from the sky and grasped for random things floating around to save himself from the dangerous fall. What used to be funny now became harrowing. I could barely watch it; I related to the falling character grabbing thin air for help. Silent tears stung my eyes again as the secret longing for life to be the way it was, filled my heart. I longed that time would go backward, so I could feel safe, feel loved unconditionally, and feel valuable. But that felt impossible, and I felt like I could tell no one. *What would happen if I did? What would happen to me? What would happen to Dad? Our family? How could Mom handle it, she was already so exhausted, and Grandma would be devastated. I have to carry this secret alone, by myself.*

I didn't see Dad until after school on the following Monday evening when he returned from work. He walked in the door that led from the garage to the kitchen. He and Grandma were having a conversation, and I was waiting to see how he would respond to me. He walked past me as if nothing had happened, which was a

24

tremendous relief to me. I followed his lead and acted as if nothing had happened.

SECRET LONGINGS

I longed for peace in my family. I wanted to feel valuable, accepted. I started being more concerned about my appearance and became interested in boys.

It was later that same summer when a friend invited me to join a neighborhood softball game her brother was forming. "I'm not that good," I warned.

"Don't worry; it's just a pick-up game for fun," she answered.

We joined everyone at the vacant lot, where they had marked out a diamond with real bases. It didn't look like just a pick-up game to me. These guys look serious.

The captains had already started picking their teams, and as we walked up, I heard. "I pick, Mimi."

My heart leaped at the thought of being chosen by a popular high school junior. But the joy was soon followed by a feeling of fear and dread knowing he would soon discover that he picked the least capable person possible for his team.

Instantly, I had a crush on him. He chose me even though he didn't have to; something in my heart lifted. After that day, he picked me every time we played. He took an interest in me and taught me how to bat and pitch. His hand would brush against mine "accidentally," and then intentionally, and then he held my hand.

"Mimi why did God make you so pretty. It's hard to concentrate when you're around," he said while we put the bats, balls, and gloves in the trunk of a friend's car.

As the kids walked away or hopped in the car, he turned to look at me and asked, "Do you mind if I walk you home?"

Feeling like the most special person on the planet, I nodded yes. As Frank and I gained distance from everyone else, he stopped and kissed me. I felt electricity flow through my body. I wanted him to kiss me again. He walked me home, and I floated into the house. From then on, thoughts of him preoccupied my mind.

HAVE YOU EVER PLAYED THE FOOL?

The summer days and nights were filled with babysitting, helping Mom at home, hanging out with friends, and thinking about Frank. Whenever there was an opportunity to be near him, I did everything I could to be there. One night his sister, Betsy, invited me to attend a sleepover. After eating pizza, drinking soda, playing games, and watching a movie, we fell asleep in her room.

In the middle of the night, I felt a tap on my shoulder. I looked up and saw a silhouette of Frank with his finger to his mouth, motioning me to be quiet. He cocked his head toward the door inviting me to come with him. My heart raced at the excitement that he wanted to spend more time with me. I slowly got out of bed and followed him. I had never been in his room before and felt very uncomfortable following him into his room. It should have been off-limits. I slowly followed him. Shutting the door, he began to kiss me. I stood there in my nightgown melting. I felt prized, chosen, and cherished.

Holding my hand, he led me to his bed. I resisted, and he calmed me down by whispering how much he loved me. The words that I longed to hear. My mind was reeling. *What if people found out that I was in his room? My reputation would be ruined!* But he kissed me again, and I melted in his arms. It wasn't long before he picked me up, laid me on his bed, and then laid on top of me. He was heavy and began whispering what he wanted to do. I wasn't *exactly* sure what he meant, but I knew it was more than I knew

26

how or wanted to do. I struggled, and he kept shushing me. Within an instant, his gym shorts were off in a flash, my nightgown was up, and he was forcing himself inside me. Piercing pain flooded my insides, I started to scream, and he put his hand over my mouth. I got quiet, and he took his hand away.

"What's the matter?" he asked impatiently.

"I can't do this!" I pleaded.

"Why not? You love me, don't you?" he reasoned.

"I can't do this," I whispered back. "Mimi, I love you," he said not too convincingly.

"Frank, I can't! "Why," he pleaded desperately.

"It hurts," I replied. "Oh, for God's sake, Mimi, go ahead then. Just go, get out of here!"

Humiliated, I crept out of his room, feeling the weight of his rejection and the shame of being in the situation. I slipped back into my friend's room, feeling mortified and ashamed.

When I woke up the next morning, I was hoping Frank would have left, but he was still there. Betsy and I headed for the kitchen to eat breakfast when I heard Frank downstairs in their basement talking to a neighbor friend who stopped by. They were laughing, and I listened intently to their conversation for fear he was talking about me and sharing what had happened the night before.

I heard the neighbor ask Frank a question, "If you had one week to live, what would you do?"

Without any delay, Frank answered confidently, "That's easy! I would f$&# as many virgins as possible."

They laughed, and my heart sunk as the truth registered in my mind, "I was one of those virgins."

Have you ever played the fool? Time stood still, and I felt paralyzed as the reality sunk in. Disbelievingly, I accepted, *He never loved me.* It seems so silly now; I was only fourteen years old. What could I have known about love? I felt hatred toward him and humiliation about the "relationship," and an urgent desire to leave.

"Betsy, I have to go. I forgot that Mom told me to be home by 10:00 a.m. She's working today, and she needs me to babysit," I lied. As I ran home, tears streamed down my face as I grasped the fact, "How could I have been so stupid! I have to pull myself together. I can't walk in the door looking like I have been crying. I can't let Mom know. I can't undo last night. I can't go back and make it different. It's done. Oh, God, I'm ruined!"

Condemnation filled my entire being. I felt like trash, but worse. I felt gross - like a used piece of tissue a person would use to blow their nose – and then throw in the trash can. I felt completely unsalvageable. *Who wants a used piece of tissue? Who would want me?*

I recognize now that I was naïve, immature, and desperate to be loved. I wanted acceptance and to be valued and affirmed. I wanted something that a high school guy who was trying to prove himself could not give. Back then, I wasn't sure how to name what happen with Frank. I came to realize that I was raped. Sure, I followed him into his room, and I wanted him to love me. But I didn't want him to do what he did. I resisted and said, "No!" That night, something very valuable was taken from me and regret immediately filled my heart. Sexual intimacy was something I wanted to be special and beautiful between the man I marry and me, but it was painful and ugly.

Life seemed to be full of booby traps. Each trap caused me to lose more parts of myself. I felt lost, and I wasn't sure how I would get back to normal.

BROKEN MARRIAGE – BROKEN FAMILY

My mom needed me that summer, which was a blessing, because I don't know how I would have survived without being kept occupied. And I was all about survival. I was starting high school, and I had to face the fact that my reputation might be beyond repair. I had one chance to make it in high school and do that one thing I had become an expert in — being nice. While hiding that I am "not good," I had to be sure to "be nice." *If I am nice, no one will have reason to hate me or mistreat me.* That was my game plan.

I struggled to focus in class and concentrate on homework. My thoughts always circled back to the unexplainable events of my life. Instead of studying, I threw myself into social activities like cheerleading, student council, and being with friends. What happened between Frank and me was never mentioned during that summer. I didn't have to face the embarrassment of my entire school knowing about that night. I kept to my plan - I was nice. No matter who you were, what people thought of you, or what you thought of me, you always got a smile from me. I made new friends, and we shared common interests – often attending football and basketball games together, sleepovers, shopping, and talking about boys.

Relief filled my heart as Mom shared that she and dad were separating.

Encouragingly, she told me, "I found a little house, and we will have a fresh start. Dad will still live here with Grandma, and you will visit him on the weekends," Mom continued.

I still had told no one about Dad. There was too much going on. Besides, Dad didn't approach me again, and I hoped the past incident wasn't going to reoccur. I wouldn't know how to describe it if someone asked, and I didn't know what would happen to Dad or me if anyone knew.

My parents' divorce forced us into poverty. When mom mentioned that we were starting over, I pictured the little house having a white picket fence lined with rose bushes and a stone path leading to the front door. When we drove up to the house, I tried to hide my disappointment from mom as the seven of us walked into the tiny two-bedroom home on the edge of a rough neighborhood. The fact that mom was hopeful and looked happy was an encouragement.

The first night sleeping at our new house, I was acutely aware that there was no man in the house. I felt vulnerable and afraid that there was no one to protect us, and for good reason. For the years that we lived there, we were greeted by peeping Toms, experienced thieves breaking in to steal the little possessions we had, and a young man who broke in one night with the intent to rape Mom. Fortunately, she scared the hell out of the guy, and he ran out. At the same time, there were nice people in the neighborhood. It was awkward to ask friends over to our house, but not nearly as embarrassing as paying for our food with food stamps.

Mom knew I was uncomfortable about them and encouraged me, "Mimi, this is temporary. Welfare is for people in crisis, and we are in a crisis. We won't be in this situation for long."

She worked hard at her entry-level position at the hospital. I don't know how she worked full time and raised six kids, but she did. Over time, she was promoted to a management position and continued in leadership and was eventually honored by winning the Leader of the Year award. A valuable gift I received from Mom was that, although our family could have fallen into a victim mindset, she never believed we were victims. She always looked for solutions to move forward.

I felt that having a boyfriend would fill every gaping hole in my heart, and it wasn't long before I began dating a guy, and we got serious fast. I was a freshman in high school, and Brad was a sophomore. Mom called Brad a silver-tongued, SOB. But I treasured every silver-coated word he spoke to me. We spent hours on the phone in the evening and our weekend nights dating or attending his football games.

He pressured me to have sex with him, "You're frustrating me. You can't kiss me and just leave me hanging."

I loved being with him, but I wasn't budging. I knew how easy things could get out of control from experience, so I set boundaries and was determined not to cross them. We dated for over a year.

Then my best friend's sister picked me up for a sleepover and dropped the bomb. "Mimi, I think you need to know something. Did you know that Brad slept with Jill last weekend?"

"What? What do you mean he slept with her?" I asked.

"He told her that he was breaking up with you because you won't sleep with him. She told him that she would sleep with him, and he spent the night at her house when her parents were out of town. Now they're dating. I just thought you should know."

My heart was pierced, and I was paralyzed. I couldn't think. I thought Brad hadn't called me because he was at a football camp. He lied to me. *When was he going to tell me?* The rejection was more than I could handle. *He never said a word to me!* It felt like someone took a stun-gun and tasered my heart. I was angry and wanted to hide my emotions but couldn't. My response was not what she had expected, and she began to apologize profusely. It was too late.

When I was with Brad, the pain in my heart left. I felt loved and accepted every time we were together. *Now, what am I going to do?* I groaned internally. Losing him was a shock. I could hardly bear the rejection and thoughts of a future without him, and the embarrassment of being dropped for someone else – someone "friendlier" - was unbearable.

"Susie, I'm not up to a sleepover tonight. Would you take me home?" I asked, trying to sound as composed as possible.

When we reached home, I ran to my room, fell onto my bed, and cried. I was confused because I was told that if you were good, guys would respect you and honor you - good, meaning refrain from having sex. But I lost the most important person to me because I was trying to be good. *I don't get it. I don't know how life works. It's impossible to figure out!* Loneliness swept over me. Acid-like pain in my chest surfaced. Life seemed to be closing in on me. When Mom came home that night, I begged her to take me to the hospital.

"Sweetheart, I can't take you to the hospital."

"But why not? I feel like I am going to explode."

"I can't, Mimi, because hospitals are for people who are sick, and you're not sick. You don't even have a fever."

No fever? I felt like a hot raging fire to me. "Mom, if I'm not sick, then why am I in so much pain?"

I fantasized about purchasing a set of expensive Waterford crystal glasses and taking them behind the school I attended. There were plenty of concrete walls there, and I wanted to throw each glass, full force, onto the concrete wall and watch them shatter into pieces. That's how I felt, shattered. Too many secrets. Too many disappointments. I was broken, with no one to help me pick up the pieces.

LIVING NIGHTMARES

At 16 years old, visiting Dad on the weekends took its toll on me. Dad renewed his advances toward me, and it became a cat and mouse game. Until one night, Dad took a stand and informed me,

32

"Mimi, you're too old to sleep with the girls. I want you to sleep on the couch from now on."

I felt awkward and dirty. *Too old? Why is it wrong for me to sleep with them?* And then I knew what he meant. If I were alone on the couch, I would be accessible.

I tried to negotiate with him and was met with a firm answer, "No. I am your father! Listen to me and obey me!"

"Can I sleep with Grandma?" I pleaded.

"Mimi, you are disobeying me!" I was intimidated by Dad and terrified to cross the line with him.

Not knowing what was *'really'* going on, Grandma brought out a sheet, pillow, and blanket, and I made my bed on the couch. Each weekend night, I tried to stay awake for as long as I could because Dad never approached me until I was asleep. Each weekend I woke up terrified because, in the dark, Dad was touching me in ways that were confusing and frightening to me. I didn't understand what he was doing and felt a sense of horror and dread each time I woke up this way. I continued to wake up Grandma with my nightmare screams, and each weekend I felt dirtier than the one before.

One Friday evening, when Dad came to pick us up to stay with him for the weekend, I overheard him tell Mom that Grandma wouldn't be home. She was visiting her elderly aunt for the weekend. I froze in terror and excused myself to go to the bathroom inside.

While everyone packed their things in Dad's car, Mom came to check on me, "Mimi, are you OK."

"Mom, I'm sick. I can't go!"

"Honey, he's your father. He only sees you on the weekends. You have to go."

"I can't, Mom. I can't."

We discussed it back and forth as I pleaded with her to let me stay home, and she became adamant, saying, "You are going, and you had better hurry because everyone is waiting on you."

Fear filled my heart, and I led Mom into the tiny bedroom, closed the door, and broke down and told her, "Mom, I can't! Dad has been touching me and stuff, and I can't do it anymore."

Mom was in shock and sat next to me. She asked several questions to understand and get clarity. I could only share with her what I understood. Many things that happened I couldn't articulate and wouldn't know until I was an adult. She was horrified, and she believed me. Terrified of what might happen, I begged her not to tell Dad that she knew. She promised me that she wouldn't say anything that day. She went out and told Dad that I was sick and that I wouldn't be able to go. I heard Dad respond impatiently and angrily. Dad and my siblings drove away, and for the first time in a long time, I felt a boulder had been lifted from my chest.

I'm not sure what happened next; I know Mom made some phone calls. It was a very delicate situation. She shared this information with my Dad's family. They related the story to Dad to find out if it was true. He replied that it was the sickest thing he had ever heard and accused Mom of making it up. Who were they supposed to believe? They stood behind Dad, and it was uncomfortably 'dropped.' It took all the courage I had to tell Mom what was happening. I was deeply hurt that they didn't believe me. Being around extended family used to be treasured times and now, with trust broken, Holidays and time spent together were awkward and something I wanted to avoid. That feeling of connectedness was gone. I didn't return to Dad's for a long time, not until he had remarried, and even then, it was not overnight.

NIGHTMARES THAT REPLACED THE NIGHTMARES

The weight of my cursed identity was crushing.

I thought I had escaped the nightmares, but now real 'nightmares' replaced the pretend ones. I fell asleep and experienced the first of a long series of terrifying and recurring dreams. I was in a secret chamber, it was dark, and I peered into my soul. I gazed happily at the beautiful, brilliant, pure, white circle. It gleamed against the darkness. Then mysteriously, a drop of black would drip from an obscure ceiling above and stain my soul. I lied a lot, it's how I got what I wanted, and in the dream, each drop of black reminded me of my lies. Drops would drip, and each drop represented an iniquity I committed. By the time my dream ended, my beautiful white soul was covered in horrifying darkness with just a pin-head size of white left.

I had one more chance to be good. If I messed up, I would be doomed to hell. Each night I panicked as I watched my soul turn from white to black and my emotions from hope to doom.

The condemning voice from the past, the voice that visited me the first night Dad attempted to abuse me, spoke to me again, "If you sin one more time, you are going to hell. That's where you belong. You belong in hell."

I woke up pleading, "God, please forgive me for all the bad things I have done. I don't want to be bad. I want to be good. I am so sorry."

But the next night, my soul turned from glistening white to death-black again. I had only one more chance to live a good life.

"I'll try to be good, God. I promise I'll try."

I was walking on eggshells, afraid to make one more mistake. A false identity was being cemented in my mind. I am bad. I have to try to make it up. It's up to me to turn things around, make them better. I have one more chance and a pin-hole size of value left.

I learned to toggle between things that would get my mind off the despair and the things that triggered it. I couldn't stay still and study, and my mind would drift to the upsetting memories. If I kept busy and active with friends and school activities, I could keep it at bay; but it came back with a vengeance when I was alone. It's funny because I often escaped despair by cleaning. Other mothers would tell my mom they wished I would rub off on their daughters or say, "Mimi, is so good!" Little did they know that it was because I felt so bad that I looked so good.

Mom had asked me to get groceries from Hamer's Market, within walking distance just up the street. It was raining out, and as I waited for the rain to stop, I sat on my bed and looked out the window that faced the back of our house into what we called "the gulley." The gulley was a property that separated our house from a very rough part of the neighborhood. The gulley was unkept with overgrown weeds and ground cover, a place where people threw things they no longer wanted. Deeply saddened, feeling alone and hopeless, I closed my eyes, and darkness visited me. It came over me like a cloak. In my mind's eye, I saw an endless black tunnel beckoning me to slide down into it. Part of me was curious about what was at the end of the dark tunnel, while part of me was terrified. A knowing thought came to me; If I *allow myself to be swallowed by this darkness, I could be locked in it forever.* Tears stung my eyes as I longed for things to be different. I was hoping for the impossible – for Mom and Dad to be reconciled, for Dad to apologize and change, for a boyfriend who loved me.

I can't explain what happened next, but as I shifted my focus from the dark tunnel and looked out the window again, the gulley was instantly transformed into a paradise. Time stood still. The colors were vivid. The sky, a comforting blue, stood guard over this sacred place. A majestic, huge rock sat to the right of a peaceful, clear stream that ran through the vibrant garden. Everything seemed alive.

36

The rock was big enough to stand on, solid enough to be secure, strong enough to be immovable, and it was beckoning me to come and sit on it.

I answered this call by saying, "I want to, but I don't know how to get to you."

The boulder felt alive, safe, and secure. I wanted to go there, to run there, to be there and live there. The vision lingered for a moment, and then it was gone. The gully returned to its original unkempt state of overgrown weeds. A notion came to me, *Mom, my brothers, and sisters! I must hold on for them. I have to stay strong for them.* My thoughts were turned from my circumstances to my future as I vowed to look forward; I *have to stay strong for Mom.*

The rain stopped, and before I grabbed the grocery list, I reflected on both visions, the beautiful, inviting landscape, and the dark foreboding tunnel.

I spoke to God, "God, if you would just give me a chance, I'll show you what I can do."

I wanted to be good enough for God. I had equated being good with being lovable and proving my worth. I wanted God's love and acceptance and thought I needed to prove to Him that I was valuable enough for Him to love me.

THE RIFLEMAN

I looked forward to watching The Rifleman after school. Each episode demonstrated a strong, protective, and morale father who went to any lengths to protect and rescue his son. He became a dream dad (and future husband) to me. Eventually, I convinced myself that the Rifleman, or someone like him, was someone I would pursue, but would never gain — I would never be good enough to deserve a 'Rifleman' of my own. My self-image and esteem were shot. I kept the dream to myself, hoping that someday there would be a man that would value me as much as the Rifleman loved his son. Someday there would be a man that would fight for me, sacrifice for me and create a safe place for me to live.

DREAMS IN THE BIG CITY

With average grades and not a great prospect for college, I shared with my high school guidance counselor that I wanted to find a way to earn money soon. She suggested that I attend a Professional Executive Assistant Certificate Program at Robert Morris University in Carthage, Illinois. Because of our economic situation, they offered me a grant that would cover tuition and I would work for them to cover school expenses. Not confident enough to pursue a bachelor's degree, Mom and I agreed this was the best option. For the first time, I was away from home. I missed my siblings. It was a cold winter that year. I did not have money to have a winter coat and wore a raincoat while walking between school buildings. Although I met one of my best friends there, I couldn't graduate fast enough. My first roommate was very troubled and tried to commit suicide. She was the first person I met that felt worse than I did. They moved me to a new room, and my second roommate was close to graduating from the Nursing Program and was busy studying for her Boards. Loneliness crept in, and I applied for the Resident Assistant position. That kept me busy and gave me a sense of purpose until I graduated.

Upon graduation, my Aunt and Uncle invited me to live with them in Chicago. It was a gracious act of love on their part to adopt a 19-year-old into their home while they had two young children to raise. Living on a tidy street of a Northern Chicago suburb where every yard was meticulously landscaped thrilled my heart. *This is really going to be a new beginning.*

Soon after I moved in, they took me downtown, where I saw the city for the first time. Moving to Chicago was a dream come true. My eyes were wide as I gaped at the incredible size of the buildings and the beauty of Lake Michigan. My heart was overwhelmed with excitement that this "really" was a new beginning for me. *No one knows me or what happened to me. I can be anyone I want to be. I will find my way here! I can be good here.*

My uncle was my godfather, I loved him dearly, and he was always loving to me. He worked as the Director of the Parks and Recreation Department in the city where we lived. My aunt was a role model to me. She was confident and supportive and helped me with my first job opportunity. My cousins were loads of fun, and their personalities created lots of laughter. I was living with a real family. We spent our evenings riding bikes on the miles of beautiful trails that run through the Chicago suburbs. The Chicago Bears won the Super Bowl that year and following the Bears with my aunt and uncle helped me feel connected to something bigger than myself.

One afternoon while helping my uncle clean out the garage, I got the courage to ask him a question.

"Uncle Dave, I know that you talked to Dad about what happened between him and me. Could you help me understand?"

Uncle Dave had a big and loving heart. I saw the pain in his eyes as he reflected on my question. I could tell that he was hesitant to answer.

"Mimi, I can't help you understand because I don't understand."

"Could you tell me what he told you?" I asked.

Again, his eyes were full of pain. Dad was his older brother. I can't imagine how he felt.

"Oh, Mimi. I don't know if this helps, and I don't know if I should even repeat it, but he told us that he was too drunk to remember," he said with a deep sadness.

"I see," I answered, "that means there are no answers."

"I guess you could say that," he responded.

"Thanks, Uncle Dave. I sincerely appreciate it."

I saw how painful this was for him and wanted to comfort him.

"I'm so sorry, Mimi," he said, and he walked over and held me.

We both cried. "Me too, Uncle Dave."

We never talked about it again. What more would there have been to say. I had not realized that Dad was drunk those nights. It was hard to accept that my Dad was so drunk that he didn't remember being part of the most terrifying times of my life. It felt wrong that Dad's life and my life were so disconnected. *How could I be so trivial to someone I loved so much?*

Troubled and wanting answers, the weekend after the conversation I had with my uncle, I drove the six-hour drive from Northern Chicago to Southern Illinois to visit Dad and ask him the question on my heart. Dad was sitting outside in his backyard smoking a cigarette when I drove up. He was surprised to see me and invited me to sit with him. He offered me something to drink, which I declined.

"Dad, I came because I need you to help me understand something," I shared with him anxiously.

"What is that, Mimi?" Dad asked inquisitively.

"Dad, can you explain why you did it?"

Afraid to look at his blue eyes, I looked down at the freshly cut lawn beneath my feet. I broke the silence by looking up at Dad. I don't know what I expected to hear from him. I just wanted some answers.

He sat back in his lawn chair and took a deep breath, "Mimi, since the beginning of time, women have caused men to sin."

It would have felt better if he had belted me in the stomach. I wanted to run but was frozen and clueless as to how to respond. I looked down, and without saying a word, I used every ounce of strength to stand up, walk toward the front of the house, get back in my blue Mustang, and drive six hours back to Chicago. *That #*&° of a *&°#%@ is blaming me!?* I couldn't control the tears as I screamed at the top of my lungs. I had felt guilt and shame. I had felt confused and worried. Now new emotions entered my heart— intense feelings of hatred, resentment, and bitterness.

Driving North on Interstate 55, I rolled down my window, stuck out my head, and screamed, "God, I hate you! What did I ever do to you to cause you to hate me so much?"

ON MY WAY

My new goal was to make friends and start a new life. Start over. Start fresh. Reinvent myself. Be a "new" me. I worked as an assistant to the Director of Human Resources at a large pharmaceutical company. I was lonely. Making friends was not as easy as I had hoped. One day a group of girls from the floor below mine were going to Greek Town for dinner and invited me. We agreed that I would meet the group in the parking lot of one of the girl's apartments in Skokie, a neighboring suburb. When everyone arrived, we drove to Greek Town together in two cars. My aunt knew I was lonely and was so happy I had an opportunity to go out with friends.

"I don't know what to wear," I confided in her.

She lent me her new beige suede suit. It fit like a glove.

41

Unfamiliar spices and smells filled the air as Greek musicians played mandolins, keyboards, and drums. We found a large table facing the band, and the girls recommended their favorite dishes to me. The music and food were a completely new experience. We chatted throughout the night and laughed as several of the girls flirted with members of the band. After eating, we asked for the bill and were ready to leave. I left cash on the table to cover my dinner and excused myself to go to the restroom. When I returned to the table, I found it empty. I rushed out to the parking lot and saw another car pulling into the spot where we were parked. My heart sunk. They forgot me! Surely, they will come back. I waited for 30 minutes and then an hour. I saw the band start packing up their instruments, and I knew what that meant. The restaurant was getting ready to close.

I was too embarrassed to call my aunt and tell her I had been left behind. We didn't have cell phones, and I didn't have these ladies' home phone numbers. With not enough money to order a cab, I began deliberating my choices and began to realize that I would have to make the painful phone call to Uncle Dave, tell him what happened, and ask him to get me. As I turned to ask an employee of the restaurant to use their phone, a handsome man approached me with thick black hair and dark eyes. He said he had been watching me in broken English and noticed that I was worried and wanted to know if I needed help. He looked compassionately at me as I explained the situation to him.

"That is no problem. No problem at all," he said. "I know what we'll do. I'll drive you home."

"Really?" I answered.

"Absolutely," he responded. His accent was foreign to me, as was the situation I was in, but he seemed like a genuinely good guy. As we stepped outside, he confidently motioned toward his car, and I felt rescued. Problem solved!

I explained that if he navigated to Interstate 94, I would guide him the rest of the way.

"OK, we just have to make one short stop on the way," he said. Now relieved, I was amazed how he traveled through the streets of Chicago with great confidence and speed.

We stopped in front of a tall apartment building. He looked over at me, saying, "I shouldn't leave you here alone. It's' not safe. Come with me. We won't be long."

I followed him into the concrete building, up the elevator, and into a dark apartment. Enough city light peered through the curtain-less window to show no pictures on the walls and that the apartment was sparsely furnished. I waited for him to turn on the lights as he motioned to me, and I followed him into the kitchen. Abruptly, he grabbed me. I wasn't sure what was happening until he put both hands on my aunt's suede jacket and forced it open, causing several buttons to rip right off.

I stood paralyzed and did whatever he demanded because I knew I was in trouble. Fear filled my mind. I was alone with a man I didn't know, somewhere in the middle of downtown Chicago. I had seconds to assess my situation. I decided not to put up a fight, not struggle, just cooperate. He threw me on the kitchen table, and he raped me.

After he was done, he ordered, "Get dressed. I'll take you home."

I prayed he was telling the truth as I scrambled in the dark for my clothes. Silently we entered the elevator and walked outside. He opened the door of his black sports car, I got in, and we drove away from the city. I contemplated jumping out of the car or running away, but I rationalized that I could place myself in even more danger. We drove in silence. When we reached the suburb, I nervously gave him directions to the apartment parking lot. Instead of walking to my car, I ran to the apartment door, so he would not know which car was mine and follow me home.

I frantically pushed the buzzer with my co-worker's last name on it. My friend had been sleeping and groggily told me her apartment number and buzzed me in. Words could hardly spill out as I relived what had just happened; my whole body was shaking. I looked down at my aunt's suit jacket and wondered how I would match the missing buttons. I don't know what I was hoping to hear from Lona, but it certainly wasn't what I heard come out of her mouth, "You deserved it. You should have known better. How could someone be so naïve?"

I stood in disbelief. My terrified heart felt the blow of her words. It felt like someone took a hammer to it.

I whispered out a request, "May I use your bathroom and stay here until morning. I don't want to wake my aunt and uncle by coming in so late."

In the bath, I tried to wipe the smell of men's cologne from my body. My tears fell into the bathwater. I filled the washcloth with soap and scrubbed as hard as possible but couldn't wash the shame away. I scrubbed and scrubbed, but to no avail. The cologne was hardly disappearing, and the disgrace of being violated wouldn't budge from my terrified heart. While drying off, I decided to leave Lona's apartment and enter quietly into my aunt and uncle's house so as not to wake them. I couldn't bear to be near her one second longer. I was in pain physically and emotionally, and I didn't know how to articulate it or with whom to share it. Looking around to make sure that the man was not around, I ran to my car and drove to my aunt and uncle's home.

I quietly slipped in the side door of the house, hoping not to wake anyone. I changed into my pajamas and tried to wash the stains from my aunt's suit. I examined where the buttons were torn off and thankfully noticed the suit was not ripped. His cologne lingered on the clothing, so I rolled it up tightly and placed it in a plastic bag. I planned to take it to the cleaners after work on Monday and hoped they would have matching buttons. Quietly, I slipped into the bed.

As I lay there, Lona's question kept tormenting me, "How could you be so naïve?" I was 19 years old, and I didn't know what naïve meant, but I was sure it meant something like "idiot." Then the haunting voice from the past, the voice I thought I had left behind, the voice that I thought belonged to God, came back confirming my assessment.

"You are bad."

"I know," I whispered. *At least he didn't call me an idiot.*

I thought about the night. How foolish I had been. I was so excited to be invited; I hadn't thought to consider who I was going with. *I don't even know these people.* I assumed that because they asked me, they cared about me and wanted to be friends. I was confused. I imagined them all laughing as they drove away from the restaurant without me. Then my thoughts began drifting toward the stupid decision I made.

I felt overwhelmingly nauseous at a terrifying thought, "What if I'm pregnant? How would I tell my aunt and uncle? How could I face them? They were so happy for me." I wanted to cry but was afraid once I started, I wouldn't stop.

I was broken, and I knew it. *Why was everyone else confident? How did they know what to do and how to fit in? How did Lona know what to do? Why was it so difficult for me? There must be something really wrong with me. I must have missed something along the way. I have to learn how to belong, how to be accepted.*

There is a language of sophistication that the world speaks, and I vowed to understand it and be a part of it. I would learn how to be on top. That was my new game plan. I would do what it took to be sophisticated. *And I will become rich so I can buy what I need to look sophisticated, and I will be famous so that people will love me.* Nothing was going to stop me. With a new game plan in place, I went to sleep.

I woke up to the smell of bacon and eggs. I heard the sound of dishes clanging and my aunt and uncle in the kitchen. *How am I going to face them? How am I going to hide how I feel?*

I pulled the blankets over my head. I felt a hardness come over my heart, and I didn't stop it. I knew that if I let the hardness take root, it would be difficult to overcome it. But I just didn't care. I decided that somehow, I was going to get what I wanted, when I wanted and how I wanted it. I remembered my new game plan and hopped out of bed.

I remained polite, just distant. I sat down at the breakfast table and looked out the window.

"How was the big night?" My uncle asked.

I smiled back and replied, "It was fine."

"What did you think of the music?" My aunt asked.

"It was different," I replied.

"Are you Ok?" they asked.

"Yes, just tired. I think I'll pass on the game today. It was a late night."

How could I share what happened? Especially with my cousins so innocently sitting there.

The humiliation of being left behind. The stupid decision to accept a ride from a stranger. Being raped! Afraid I was going to be murdered and dumped in the middle of Chicago! Humiliated by Lona's words. And possibly carrying a baby from a stranger!!! *What would they think of me? Would they regret inviting me to live with them?* I kept it to myself.

We cleared the table, finished washing the dishes, and they drove off. I was left alone – and that's when I felt it – the same pain I felt before – but more intense - the same acid-like pain in my chest when Dad abused me, when Frank forced himself on me, and when Brad dumped me. *I should have gone with them*, I lamented.

Tightness grew inside, and my chest began to burn with pain. I got dressed and went outside for a walk. The walk turned into a jog, and then I picked up speed and ran into an all-out sprint. I tried to outrun the pain. Maybe, if I run fast enough, I could get relief for just a few seconds, but the pain was impossible to escape. And running became my new therapy. I began to run every day; One mile a day, then two, then five. I was trying to escape. No matter how hard or long I ran, the pain stayed. But I kept running anyway.

SEEKING ANSWERS IN ALL THE WRONG PLACES

To learn the world's ways, my first tutors were Cosmopolitan and Glamour. I just had to look at the models' pictures to be convinced that *they* hold the answers, Beautiful women, perfect faces, perfect bodies, perfect personalities. They were desired. They were confident. To understand how life works, I also listened intently to the lyrics of the latest pop hit. I memorized the lines. I studied actresses to learn how to talk, carry myself, and dress. I became a people watcher. The answer was somewhere out there, and I wanted to be a part of it. I hated living on the outside. I wanted to live on the inside where all the beautiful, happy, confident people lived. *Where are those people you see having fun on the*

47

billboards? How do you get invited to the parties you see in the ads and the magazines?

At the same time, I was angry. I was hurt. I felt lost. It was at this point in my young life that I began looking for affection. I longed to be held and threw good judgment out the window. I felt emotionally bankrupt. I compromised to be held by someone who loved me—and suffered the horrible emotional consequences of being used.

I moved into an apartment with two roommates 25 miles west of my aunt and uncle's home. I had started a part-time waitressing job and would soon be starting a new day-time job as well. I had to make a fresh start again. It was Thanksgiving, and I didn't have enough gas money to make the trip home to be with my family, so I offered to work the Holiday weekend waitressing. I was 20 years old, and this was the first Holiday I spent without family or friends. Thanksgiving night was difficult. It seemed that the entire apartment complex was vacant, and I felt very vulnerable and alone. The first night of the holiday weekend, I double-checked the locks on the door, jammed a sturdy chair under the door handle, and tried to sleep, but to no avail.

No matter what I tried, I couldn't sleep. In those days, the only thing on late-night TV was boxing or a Christian evangelist. I chose boxing, but I couldn't stand the sight of watching the men beat each other. Grudgingly, I switched the channel and watched a woman wearing big hair with mascara running down her face from crying. She was talking about how much Jesus loves us. *Oh brother.* She looked bizarre to me. I couldn't believe I was watching this, but I would surely throw up if I watched one more round of boxing. A man started talking, "I know that there is someone watching tonight who is feeling pain in their chest. You have gone to doctors, and they don't have any answers." I felt myself sit up. He was getting my attention. "The pain you are feeling is not from a disease; it's emotional. You suffered some kind of trauma, and you need God's healing touch." Well, that must not be me, I thought. I didn't suffer any trauma (as if being sexually abused as a child and raped as a young adult wasn't traumatic). I prayed the prayer that he suggested anyway and asked God that if he were real, would He come to visit me or help me know Him? Then I fell asleep.

On Monday, I started my new day job at Motorola. When I arrived there, I was greeted by Millie, the person who would be training me. Her smile was welcoming. I felt at ease with her immediately. She was beautiful, confident, and competent. Millie befriended me. There was just something about her that made me feel that this really was going to be a new beginning.

My roommates were Delta flight attendants and required to relocate to Atlanta. I was forced to look for a new place to live. Millie introduced me to her sister, Helen. Helen and I became best friends and roommates. Helen was the most unique person I had ever met. Helen was refreshing. She was fun and accepting. She was kind and encouraging.

I asked Helen, "Why are you so different from everyone else? You are kind, and you aren't looking to gain anything from anyone. You sincerely like people."

"If I am different, it's not because of my doing. It's because of Jesus."

I didn't understand the connection between Jesus, Helen, and Millie. I wasn't sure how I felt about God. But I was grateful to have them in my life.

I loved Helen. She laughed at innocent things and sincerely cared about me. She was genuine, transparent, and honest. I could tell her anything, and she would still accept me. While we were roommates, Helen visited me at Houlihan's, where I was waitressing and reconnected with a co-worker she knew from high school. They fell in love.

MR. HIGH SOCIETY

One late night, a man walked into Houlihan's. I'll call him Mr. High Society. He was older than me. He had beautiful blue eyes, brown wavy hair, and "was he just flirting with me?"

One of the waitresses warned me to stay away from him because "He'll break your heart."

But I already had a broken heart, and no one else was interested in me, so I began to flirt back. It wasn't long before he asked me out. I was smitten. He owned his own house, he had a prestigious job, his parents were wealthy, and he liked me. Back then those were qualifications enough in my book. We got serious very fast. He asked me to move in with him, and in my mind, that was just as good as asking me to marry him.

Helen and Millie strongly urged me to avoid the relationship. They reminded me that living with and being intimate with a man with no commitment and outside of marriage would be a big mistake.

"Mary Ann, what assurance do you have from him? This kind of relationship rarely works. You must reconsider. And it's not according to God's design – this could create a wedge between you and God," they cautioned me.

I felt there was already a wedge between God and me. As I shared what Helen and Millie had said with Mr. High Society, he made fun of them and gave me an ultimatum, "You either get Jesus and them, or you get me. You pick!"

I weighed my options: Helen is engaged. Millie is married. I am alone. *Jesus is not here. I don't know for sure if he really exists, and if he does, I won't see Him until I die. Mr. High Society is here. He loves me. And the pain in my chest is gone—I'm going with Mr. High Society!*

It wasn't long before he consumed my full attention. He included me in his life. We traveled to Vegas and the Bahamas. He showed me his stomping grounds, which included casinos, strip joints, and bars. We barbecued steaks on his deck. We partied with his friends on the weekend. I felt included and valued, and I had entered the "sophisticated" life I wanted. "I had made it!"

I was living a lifestyle that had always eluded me. I had newfound freedom. We partied each weekend with professional people, surgeons, lawyers, and successful businesspeople. Snorting cocaine from designer snuffers and drinking from crystal glasses into the night, just like the billboards and the magazine ads. I didn't know there would be a cost to this lifestyle, and it didn't take long before I became addicted to false love and false comforts. Mr. High Society became abusive, and my "sophisticated" life was beginning to fall apart.

Enamored with the feeling I had "made it," I was blind. Being attracted to this lifestyle, I made so many irresponsible choices.

After three years, I had become dependent upon Mr. High Society. He threatened to break off the relationship. I begged him to keep trying. I was a mess! I depended on him for the fake security, the bogus status he represented to me, and the empty lifestyle established in a counterfeit love. Why I was attracted to stay with someone who verbally, emotionally, and sexually abused me, I don't completely understand, with the exception I thought he was the only person that I thought would be with me. I felt, be with him or be alone. And I was terrified of being alone.

The truth was surfacing – the truth that drugs, alcohol, cigarettes, whatever crutch I was using, eventually wore off and came with heartrending consequences. What goes up must come down, and the downs were so painful I couldn't possibly describe them all on paper. The highs of cocaine felt like I was invincible but coming down was worse than you can imagine when the highs wore off. First of all, you can't stop the lows from coming, and you can't control them. You careen down, and it feels like you are in a tunnel of confusion, hopelessness, despair, and torture. Coming down from a Saturday night full of cocaine and scotch, I would punch myself in the face or twist my skin until it burned. I would run at top speed into a brick wall.

I hated myself. I saw cuss words written in my mind. Demonic faces would spring in front of me. It was a living nightmare. I was clinging to the person and lifestyle from which I should have been running. Monday morning, I convinced myself I would never do it again, but by Thursday, we were planning another weekend of partying. After three years, what I thought was a disastrous crisis, but what was most likely an answer to someone's prayer, Mr. High Society dropped me. He had found my replacement. I wasn't good enough for him anymore. Somebody else was. My heart sunk. I was discarded and could hardly breathe as I sat in my blue Mustang outside of his house, not knowing what to do. I was rejected. I was alone, wounded, friendless because everything revolved around Mr. High Society.

Fortunately, through work, I found someone looking for a roommate and moved my belongings into her apartment. With no one to help, I moved in by using sheets and blankets to slide heavy furniture and oversized boxes. I was angry and broken. *What was I going to do?* The scariest part was being alone. I was in denial. I didn't want to admit to myself how much I had compromised to fill that lonely spot in the middle of my soul. If my heart had hardened before, it was becoming a rock now.

THE BREAK BEFORE THE BREAK

Without money to buy cocaine and expensive alcohol, I fortunately stopped that lifestyle. I started a job working for an attorney in a large graphics company located in a skyscraper in downtown Chicago overlooking Lake Michigan. My boss, Mr. Grell, the Vice President and General Counsel, was planning to retire and took me to lunch before he left.

"What are your goals, Mary Ann?" he asked.

At the age of 24, I replied, "my goals really don't matter, Mr. Grell."

"Why is that?" he asked.

"Because I don't have a college degree, and I live paycheck to paycheck. My goals would require a degree and money," I answered.

"I'm curious. What is it that you want to do?" he asked more persistently this time.

"I want to own my own business," I shared with him fearfully. I had never shared my dream of owning my own business with anyone.

It was 1982, and there weren't a lot of women-owned businesses. I was ready for him to tell me to keep doing what I was doing, but he didn't.

He said, "You're bright and a hard worker. Your dream is not impossible. You need a need."

"A what?" I asked.

"A need," he responded, "businesses are built on needs. When you find a need that you can fill, you can own your own business. Start small and work smart, grow from there." He was kind and a successful person. He had confidence in me, and he gave me hope.

After Mr. Grell retired, his replacement came. His name was Jack Amber, and he was rude, demanding, and insensitive. After taking dictation, my new boss asked me to come behind his desk to look at the accompanying charts. As I walked back to look at the charts, he pulled me down on his lap. As I struggled to get up, the President of the company stepped in. I was flushed with embarrassment, Mr. Amber released his grip on me, and I walked swiftly out of the office. I was sure the President would have a "talking to" with Mr. Amber. But that didn't happen. The President got my name from Human Resources, called me that weekend, and asked if I would like to join him for dinner. My heart sunk. I told him I had plans and began looking for a new job in the suburbs. *Why is this happening? Why does everyone want to use me?*

I never felt that I was attractive. My self-image was that I was awkward, immature, definitely not pretty. I had no idea that I was young, attractive, had a contagious smile, and very naïve—the perfect blend for predators.

I quit that job and found a new job selling new and innovative technology, satellite communications equipment. Little did I know that my break would come sooner than later.

Six months into my new career of selling commercial and residential satellite equipment, I went to work and tugged on a locked door. A sign had been posted from inside the door that read, "CLOSED. OUT OF BUSINESS." Following behind me were the technicians. All of us had no idea the business was having financial trouble and had lots of questions, "Will we receive our paychecks? Is this closing permanent?" *Wow, I didn't see that coming. How am I going to make the rent?*

It was early in the morning, and we all agreed to meet at the local diner for coffee and discuss it. During that conversation, the chief technician, Mark, brought up the fact that customers bought satellite systems that we had not yet installed.

"Oh, no. Those are my customers." I was reminded of the promises that I had made. "People bought this equipment because they trusted me!" I moaned with concern.

Mark shared an idea. If the company gave us the customer list, we could start our own company. *A need! I have a need that I can fill!*

I contacted the majority owner of the company at his home, and he confirmed there was no money for payroll, but he would give us the customer list at no cost. It ended up being more valuable than the two-weeks' pay owed to us. Mark and I started a new business as partners. He would run technical operations, and I would run sales and marketing. To my delight, these circumstances created a promise of a more permanent relationship between him and me: a business and a boyfriend. I turned up the radio and flew home.

I was so excited that I didn't see the flashing lights following me down the street. While stopping at a red light and singing my lungs out, I saw a police officer impatiently standing outside my door. I turned off the radio and wound the window down.

"I have been following you for over a mile! You're 15 miles over the speed limit!" he exclaimed.

I confessed that I had lost my job but got a new opportunity and was so excited I had the radio blaring and was singing at the top of my lungs. He said that was the first time he heard that excuse, laughed, and gave me a warning. *This opportunity is really and truly a new beginning.*

It was an exciting time. The business grew fast. Sales were consistent. We had crews installing and servicing satellite and cable systems throughout the Northern and Western suburbs.

A pattern had been developed. Even though Mark and I stayed together for many years, it was a dysfunctional on-and-off relationship. Drugs and alcohol were prevalent, which distorted the relationship even more.

I didn't understand my value. Not being alone was more important than being respected. I gave too much too soon. I didn't wait to see if I would be treated well. I just jumped in. And when healthy standards were broken and healthy boundaries crossed, I accepted it, thinking that somehow, I could make it better and change the relationship or the person. Whether it be a romantic relationship or a friendship, I asked nothing from the other person. There were no commitments, only hope that everything would turn out OK.

The bad habits from my past resurfaced. Smoking two packs of Marlboro Lights a day, drinking Bacardi and Coke until I fell asleep at night, and continuing the weekend cocaine habit, depression was setting in. I began to pray, "God, please help me win the lottery." I fantasized about winning the lottery, leaving a boatload of money for mom, purchasing an endless supply of cocaine, locking myself into a hotel room somewhere, and snorting the drug until I died. That was my solution, money, and death.

Mark and I continued to struggle, and the effects partying had on us were too obvious to deny. We argued, it impacted our employees, and we wasted our money away with nothing to show. We made a conscious effort to try to make better decisions. We stopped doing cocaine and stopped drinking hard liquor – drank only beer and wine on the weekends. It was easier for Mark than for me. I felt the pull every Thursday to snort cocaine and get high, and then it stopped. I just stopped desiring cocaine. (I wouldn't understand how I was able to stop doing drugs so easily until many years later.)

I was 27 years old when I went home for Mother's Day and met one of my sisters for lunch. We met at a restaurant located next to her office. Her boss was also a pilot and flew for their employer. He entered the restaurant and walked over to say hello. He shared with my sister that he was looking for a particular plane to purchase for the company and couldn't find the model that the owner of the company requested. He appeared frustrated.

In Chicago, part of my business was installing data systems, so I asked her boss what system he was using to track that information.

"There is no system. Just a monthly pamphlet from the FAA," he shared disappointedly.

I shared that new technology enabled databases to share information in real-time.

"Well, if anyone ever created that in the corporate aircraft industry, they would be a millionaire," he exclaimed!

A need! I have found a critical need—and a way to get rich!

I drove back home exhilarated and began researching the industry and technology needed. With the help of Mark and his friend Don, I developed a business plan and prototype.

My sister's boss introduced me to a businessman in Omaha, NE, who committed to a $200,000 investment in this new business. At 28 years old, I moved to Omaha and began to build the database. We hired a research manager, administrative assistant, and part-time staff to create the database of corporate aircraft details. I took my business plan to my new accountant and attorney in hopes of finding more investors.

They agreed that it was a lucrative opportunity. They both gave advice, we improved the business plan, and we began to share it with venture capitalists. Within six months, a group of investors from Upstate New York agreed to invest the full amount needed. They were willing to invest $800,000 in the company. They flew into Omaha and completed their due diligence, and bought out the Omaha, NE investors. The conditions were that their group of investors own 80% and I owned 20% and that I would move to their city in Upstate New York to run the company under their supervision. At 29 years old, my dreams were taking flight.

MY BIG BREAK

This business became my life, and I worked tirelessly to build and maintain it. I thought the company's success would be the pinnacle of my life. Once this high-tech start-up was profitable, I would be the happiest person on the planet. I would finally be validated. At that time material success was foundational to my self-worth and identity. In 1987, women-owned businesses were few and far between. The company's success and financial security was my solution and would be the answer to my well-being. I wouldn't need anyone. I could build a fence around myself where no one could hurt me. For the first time, I would be free from pain. My plan looked like it was all coming together, except for one thing, the acid-like sting still burned in my chest.

Naively, I thought I was moving to New York City. It was an overcast Saturday evening when I drove into the small, depressed town in Upstate New York, my heart sunk. *Oh no! What did I just agree to?*

Monday morning brought its own surprises when one of the owners added a salesperson to the staff without talking with me. Lydia worked in aircraft sales and seemed to be a perfect fit. Six months after she arrived, Lydia announced that she was dating the investor and that he had bought the company for her. He planned on finding a way to force me out. It felt like someone punched me in the stomach. I confronted the investor, and he attacked me by saying I was hard on her and she was sharing this fib out of frustration. I realized that he was protecting himself – Lydia was not his girlfriend; she was his mistress. Confronting him was the best thing I could have done. Now he knew I knew about the plan and his secret relationship.

The investors had conflicts that they couldn't resolve, so one investor bought out the rest. I did not realize how vulnerable that would leave me. I was now no longer equal partners with a group of investors; I was a minority partner. And that majority owner

58

partner was unstable. He suffered from depression and would leave for months at a time, only to return very upset with decisions I made. At the same time, the company gained such a prominent place in the marketplace that our competitor tried unsuccessfully to sue us to remove us from the game.

This opportunity brought me the things that I dreamt would make me happy. I was 31, working in my designer office with my designer clothes, driving my designer vehicle. I lived in a charming historic home overlooking the farm-covered hills of beautiful Upstate New York. How I wish my life could have been as blissful as it appeared. I was supposed to be on top of the world, but I was lonely and wounded. A fear resided in my heart that I could not remove, and it manifested in bizarre ways. There were times that I was terrified to enter my home alone at night. I lived convinced that something or someone was hiding behind the bushes or the door waiting to attack me.

The majority owner asked for a working weekend meeting at his second home in the Adirondack Mountains. I thought the other board members would meet us there, but it was just him and me. He hit on me, and I was sick. He was twice my age and married. I tried to be polite and share that I was committed to Mark. The working weekend uncomfortably ended early, and I drove home that Saturday evening, fearful of the consequences of the weekend events. I decided that the best thing was to throw myself deeper into my work. I woke up at 5:00 a.m. the next morning and took the shortcut to the office. As I drove down the backroads, I stopped at a four-way stop and noticed a car that looked like Mark's parked in front of someone's house. *That's peculiar. I wonder why Mark would be there?* I asked him about it, and he blew it off, saying he was up late playing cards with friends. It wasn't long before I discovered that Mark was up late, but he wasn't playing cards. He was having an affair with one of my employees.

My heart dropped. Mark's betrayal was like a slap in the face. The embarrassment of Mark cheating on me with one of my employees stung my heart. I didn't know what to do with myself or where to go. Do I confront him or go to work? I was humiliated knowing my boyfriend was sleeping with the girl with the very, very short skirt, the very, very low top, and the big, glossy lips – sitting at a desk 20 feet from my office.

To add to the unraveling, a client called me on my home phone, "Mary Ann, there is something you need to know about your partner."

My heart dropped. *What now?*

"He is from a prominent New York Crime Family." *What!?* I was in shock! He continued, "I suggest you find someone to fill your shoes and get away from there."

Rick was a respected businessman in the industry. He was very supportive of me and helped me to connect with important people throughout the industry. He introduced me to bankers, insurance companies, aircraft manufacturers, and dealers. I became close with Rick, his wife, and his family. I trusted him. *Now what do I do?*

I pressed on with the day-to-day challenges, harboring heart wrenching concerns about every aspect of my life. Lonely, suffering from burnout, disappointment, my heart burned and yearned for something that was beyond my grasp. One bright, sunny, day while gazing out my office window, viewing the scenic foothills of the Adirondack Mountains, I realized that I was 900 miles from my family, the people I loved the most, and whispered, *This isn't it. I don't know if I am safe. There's got to be something else. But, this company is my heartbeat and my responsibility, and there is no one else who will love it and be as dedicated to it as I am.*

Later that year, the majority owner died unexpectedly of a heart attack. It was a shock to everyone. His son had recently graduated from law school and was now executor of his father's estate. He was a newlywed and announced that he would soon be returning home and would be involved in leading the company. As a relatively small company, I knew that there was not enough room for both of us at the top. I tried to justify that this was some sort of sign that I could leave, and the company would be in hands that cared about it.

The fact was that the town was small; I was lonely, my heart longed for family, community, and love. I visited my attorney to ask if the owner's son could decide to lead the company. My attorney laid the cards on the table. "You are a minority owner. You had autonomy while Vinny was alive, but that will most likely change. Since he bought-out the investors, this company is more like a family-owned business. If you and the owner's son can work things out equitably, then stay. Personally, if you were my daughter, I would recommend you make an offer to him to buy you out and start over. These situations rarely work well; he holds the cards. I trust you will have plenty of opportunities ahead of you."

After conceiving the idea of a technology company servicing high-end dealer networks, developing the business plan, acquiring the capital, moving the company out of state twice, recruiting the team to build the database and design the software, traveling throughout North America to sell and market the service, and giving my heart and soul to this company for over four years, I started to doubt myself again.

At 32 years old, I announced to my employees and clients that I decided to sell my portion of the company to the new majority owner and move back to my hometown in Illinois. Employees and customers were stunned; clients called and counseled me that I should stay, which caused me to second guess my decision. I didn't want to leave the company, the employees, and the clients, and yet I didn't know how to stay and make it work. I had the confidence to build it, but I didn't have the confidence to fight for myself staying in it, and it sounded like it wouldn't have mattered. By being a minority owner, I had little choice.

WHO TOUCHED ME?

I drove to my home in Upstate New York that night, rushed up the stairs, fell on my bed, and sobbed. I had held back tears for many years. Owning my own company, being financially stable and independent was my solution to life's problems. Now with no real solution in sight, I was overcome with fear. *What did I do? What am I going to do now?* The acid-like sting in my chest continued to burn. I had been to doctors, psychologists and counselors. Nothing and no one could help explain where the pain came from and how to get rid of it.

With another painful and unfulfilled chapter closing, and not knowing what the future would hold, I grieved and sobbed hysterically, *I can't do this anymore! I can't keep screwing up. Why can't I figure things out? Why can't I get rid of this pain?*

The uncertainty was crushing, and I began to rationalize, *I could have stayed with the company. I could have made it work! Everyone said I was crazy to leave now! What's wrong with me?! I don't know the answers. I have never known the answers.* An old familiar feeling appeared. The floor beneath my feet felt like it gave way, again. *Did I just play the fool again? Did I just give away my ticket to wealth and freedom?*

I had been crying for what seemed to be hours, I didn't know how to stop, and in the midst of this breakdown, I was touched. Literally, touched! As my face was buried in my tear-soaked pillow, a hand touched my shoulder. It startled me because I was alone. The touch felt like 'liquid love,' and it didn't stop at the surface of my skin. The touch went right through my skin and warmed my chest, where the pain dwelt. For a moment, the aching disappeared. I was caught up in the beautiful warmth of the touch. Even though it was warm and loving, there was a power behind it like nothing I had experienced. Realizing that I was alone and that someone or something I couldn't see was touching me caused me to shrink back in terror. I stirred up enough courage to look back over my shoulder to catch a glimpse, but no one was there. The liquid love withdrew, and the pain reappeared, but I felt different.

I cried out to this invisible visitor, "Please come back. Please tell me who you are!"

The visitor didn't appear. I heard no answer but felt a sense of peace and a twinge of hope.

Surprisingly, the words, "I'm going to be OK," flowed from my mouth. I felt the impact of words drop down into my heart. I whispered again, "I'm going to be OK," and fell into a deep sleep.

RETURNING HOME

When I landed at the St. Louis Airport, Mom and my siblings greeted me. They welcomed me home with wide open arms and loving hearts. At 33 years old, having been away from home since I was 18, I moved in with Mom. Mark and I were still trying to make things work. He joined me in St. Louis later, and we tried to start over—again.

I thought getting married would fix things, as if walking down an aisle in a beautiful, white wedding dress and repeating the words, "I do," would magically make every dream come true and everything OK. I hoped that one ceremony would undo years of difficulty and wounds. The length of our marriage lasted less than the time it took to plan it. I felt like I let everyone down. They invested so much to make the wedding nice. Vows had been made and gifts given. *How do I unravel the mess I made?*

Before the marriage ended, even though I was discouraged and doubtful, I tried to make it work. I was scheduled to start working for a global training company in St. Louis on a Monday. Mark was working on a job in Ohio installing a cable system in a hotel. I thought it would be good to spend time together before I started my new career. I left the prior Thursday to drive from our house

63

on the Illinois/Missouri border to his job site in Ohio. When I arrived, we worked together installing cables at the hotel.

"This is how we started," I shared as we installed cable lines together.

"Yep, it's true," he responded.

Sunday came soon, and I left early that morning to be home in time to prepare for my first day of work.

It was a hot day and on Interstate 70 somewhere in the middle of Indiana when on my way home, a tractor-trailer had overturned. Traffic was backed up for miles. Finally, the wreck was cleared, and the pace picked up when out of nowhere, a loud "boom" sounded, and my gas pedal stopped functioning. I steered to the side of the road, which was fortunately near an exit. Two helpful guys pulled over and offered to push my car down the exit to a nearby gas station.

I did not have a mobile phone and asked the gas station attendant if I could use his phone. I called Mark to discuss my options and tried to hide the tears stinging my eyes when I heard his response. Profanities filled my ear as Mark vented his feelings about what this was going to cost us.

"Do you know what this means?" he asked, exasperated.

"Not quite. What does it mean?" I asked.

"Because of this we're not getting the @%*#ing fishing boat!"

The writing on the wall couldn't have been clearer. I was alone in the middle of Indiana with a dead car, and my husband was worried about his fishing boat.

The attendant could surmise what had happened and asked, "You got AAA?"

"Yes," I answered.

"That's good. You are going to need it."

Once again, I found myself in the middle of circumstances that bewildered me. I vowed that as soon as I settled into my new career in St. Louis, I would move to an apartment and begin divorce proceedings.

I couldn't hold back the tears as we drove toward the Illinois border. The AAA driver was very understanding and shared he was a Christian and would be praying for me. After what happened later that night, I believe he did.

After returning home from the 2½ hour drive, anxiety-ridden, chain-smoking Marlboro Lights, trying to calm myself with a glass of wine, I sat in my backyard overlooking the small, peaceful, and beautiful lake and reflected on my life. I wanted to make it great, but in reality, I felt like I was a pinball in a pinball machine, bouncing from one crisis to another.

SEARCHING FOR SIGNIFICANCE & MEANING

I yearned for significance and meaning and sought it in many ways.

I sought answers in life through many relationships. And once again felt abandoned, rejected, and alone.

I sought answers through my accomplishments by building two successful businesses, working out, and running 5Ks, but felt perpetually empty.

Throughout my young adult years, I sought answers through experiences. I studied all that was considered glamorous and successful in the world. I played the party scene. I carried New Age crystals in my pocket. I repeated my daily positive affirmations that were taped to my bathroom mirror. I meditated to music with water sounds. I hosted psychic parties, was hypnotized, had my palms read, and read my horoscope every morning. I studied Ancient American Indian rituals and hung up my dream catchers. And found no answers and no meaning.

I sought answers by acquiring knowledge. I devoured a 33-Volume Time Magazine Book Set on the Hidden Mysteries of Life and read endless articles on Eastern Religions. I tried to follow and learn from the cultural gurus - Oprah, Dr. Phil, Marianne Williamson, Deepak Chopra, Stephen Hawking. I religiously visited the library and read books on entrepreneurship. I voraciously consumed INC Magazine, People Magazine, USA Today, and the Wall Street Journal. But didn't have any meaningful solutions or feel any wiser.

I sought answers through counseling and visited with therapists in every city I lived in from when I was 19 years old. Some offered helpful coping skills, while others—not. Still, there were no answers. The pain in my chest remained, and I felt a deep sense of hopelessness. I didn't want to know how to fit in anymore. I wanted the truth. I yearned for it. I had witnessed the lies, the fake lives. I was sick of the world. I was sick of life. *There has got to be something more significant.*

Although I didn't have any answers, I had questions that needed to be answered. Questions that brewed silently inside my soul until they finally came to the surface: *What is real? What is important? What is true?*

I was sitting alone on my deck. It was a clear sky, full of stars. I was literally at the end of my rope, and in total desperation and despair, from the depths of my being, I cried out loud to the sky:

"WHAT IN THE HELL IS REAL?"

"WHAT'S IMPORTANT?"

"WHAT'S THE TRUTH!?"

The night sky remained quiet, but something brewed up from the depths of my being. As if in response to my plea for understanding, a prayer I had committed to memory during my childhood welled up from within me, out of my mouth, and onto my lips ... it wasn't intentional, and even though I was confused by what I was experiencing, I spoke the words out loud.

Our Father ... *I don't want a father.*

Who art in Heaven ... *Heaven isn't real.*

Hallowed be thy name ... *I don't even know what hallowed means.*

Thy kingdom come ... *Is this some kind of fairy tale?*

Thy will be done ... *Will I lose my freedom?*

On earth, as it is in heaven ... *Does that mean I will just sit on clouds all day?*

Give us this day our daily bread ... *Is that just bread, or does it include that green dress with the sleek side pockets I saw at Marshall Field's?*

And forgive us our sins ... *Is it possible?*

As we forgive those who have sinned against us ... *Impossible.*

And lead us not into temptation ... *Why would you lead anyone into temptation?*

But deliver us from evil ... *How?*

For thine is the kingdom …

And the power …

And the glory … *Can you hear me?*

Amen.

The Truth

Monday, I woke up early without a working car. All rental companies were closed on Sundays (it was the 90s), but I found that Rent-A-Wreck was open. They were nearby and offered to drop the "wreck" off to me first thing that morning.

Nervous about my new beginning, I was anxious and full of anticipation as I started my first day at my new career. I arrived at the Monday morning meeting, took my seat in the back of the room, and before long, I was in the flow of meeting with local businesses and assisting in delivering training to my new clients. As soon as possible, I found an apartment close by and moved out to start the divorce process and a new beginning on my own.

Within a few months, I settled into my new role. I had been self-employed for almost ten years and was surprised by how quickly I adjusted to being an employee. Sometimes it felt like I was leaving luggage behind or didn't know what to do with the extra time on my hands, but I enjoyed not having the pressures and demands of owning and running a company.

I was surprised by how much I enjoyed the training industry. My new co-workers were excited about what they did and were devoted to helping people grow and develop. My clients were excited to see the results that the training brought to their lives, and I grew in confidence. People's lives were being changed, including mine.

I was used to working with challenging circumstances, unrealistic expectations, and seven-day workweeks. This environment was different. The people were different. First, their language was polite and void of cussing and crude comments. They worked collaboratively and had positive attitudes. Mistakes were seen as learning and development opportunities. People were genuinely interested in each other. I sensed that this was indeed a new beginning. Different than the other new beginnings.

One of the people I worked with was confident and successful. He was available to help people on the team that were new or struggling. So, I asked Tom if he would accompany me to client meetings when I lacked the knowledge or experience to answer their questions. In return, I assisted him as he delivered training to my clients.

Tom and I facilitated a training session at a telecommunications company west of St. Louis. Afterward, we stopped for dinner, and after conversing about the day's session, we talked about more personal topics. I confided in Tom that I was in the beginning stages of a divorce. He asked if there was a possibility of reconciliation.

"No, there's not," I answered, and hesitantly I confessed, "I take responsibility. I am the one who pushed the idea of getting married. I thought getting married would make things better, and we found out quickly that it didn't."

"Have you reached out to anyone to get help?" he asked.

"Not together. And getting help is out of the question. We tried for years. I went to counseling a lot, and he didn't at all. We just should have remained friends, but I thought getting married would somehow improve our relationship."

I changed the subject by asking more questions about the training sessions that transpired that day.

When I was a young girl, I vowed that I would never get divorced. I remember thinking, "I hate divorce!" And here I was in the middle of one. Divorce is awful. It represented a fracture to me. When my parents got divorced, our family was broken beyond repair. Nothing was the same again. There is no easy way or a friendly way to go about it. I felt a deep sense of failure, angst, and regret. At the same time, I was looking forward to the process being over. We owned the house we had lived in, a rental home, a boat, and a dog together. We were also partnering in a business. I wanted a clean break and left those things behind.

Being near family was helpful. Mom always supported me. My siblings loved and supported me with kindness and understanding. Life goes on.

WHAT, LOVE DOESN'T WORK FOR YOU?

My new apartment was sparsely furnished, but it was a start. I sat out on my patio and smoked cigarettes like a chimney, dreaming of a better future.

Tom and I had dinner again after another long training session. Inquisitively, Tom asked me my thoughts on spiritual matters, "Are you a person of faith?"

"I'm not sure what you mean," I responded, "I don't know how I feel about things like that," I answered, "I mean, I guess I believe there is a God. I want to believe there is a God. I can't think of another answer as to why we are here."

Then he asked me what my thoughts were about Jesus. I was caught off guard by Tom's question. *Not Jesus. This guy's cute and everything. I would never have guessed he was one of "those" people.*

I looked across the table and felt irritated as I thought of my past experiences, and I challenged Tom by saying, "You know, honestly, when I was a little girl, I tried Jesus ... and found that Jesus just doesn't work."

I thought that Tom would get the hint and drop the conversation, but he looked at me curiously and asked, "So, *love*, doesn't work for you?"

I glared down at the silverware, trying to hold back the tears. Love was the secret longing of my soul and something that continually escaped my grasp. "What does Jesus have to do with *love?*" I asked suspiciously.

Tom sat still for a moment before he answered, "Mary Ann, you can search the world, and you can research every religion, and you will never find a God that willingly left his throne, became a man, allowed himself to be rejected, beaten, mocked, and nailed naked to a tree, left to die, only to redeem those very people to Himself. *Jesus* has everything to do with love." Tom spoke with confidence.

Something inside my heart felt compassion toward Jesus. *It seems unfair that someone who is innocent would endure all that for people who don't want Him.*

Tom continued empathetically by saying, "Mary Ann, I don't know who hurt you, but I do know it wasn't Jesus."

How did he know I was hurt? Then I asked him the question I had always wondered, "If Jesus has everything to do with love, then why did he allow bad things to happen to me?"

He responded compassionately, "Mary Ann, Jesus didn't do those things to you and He didn't want those things to be done to you. Broken, wounded, and lost people did those things. If you run from Jesus, you're running from the only person who can heal you from those experiences."

Again, his words touched my heart, and I thought back to the warm and loving touch I felt that night in New York when I was in despair over leaving my company. *Could that have been Jesus?* If that was Him, I wanted to know.

"I'll try Him," I told Tom.

Tom and I had many more conversations after that. He gave me a book about heaven to read. I became ever increasingly curious about Jesus. The only prayer I knew was the one I recited on my deck months before. "Our Father, who art in heaven, hallowed be thy name..." And I continued to pray it daily.

Things began to shift. I was no longer preoccupied with being wealthy, famous, trying to protect myself. By working in the training industry, I started focusing on the needs of others. As I interacted with people on a deeper level, I recognized that I was not alone. Many other people had struggles of their own, some of them similar to mine.

Reflecting, I realized that something shifted when I screamed to the night sky, searching for what was real, what was important, and what was true. I had tried to get what I wanted when I wanted it and how I wanted. Finally, at the end of my rope, I realized that what I wanted, when and how I wanted it wasn't working. Was it coincidence, or did God answer me and place that prayer in my heart? That was yet to be seen. For now, it appeared I was walking on a new path, a true new beginning.

Tom and I worked on several training programs together, and I liked him. He was different than other men I had known or worked with. He had a passion for helping people and protected the underdog. I appreciated what I was learning from him during the training sessions we delivered.

Our clients were happy with the training we were conducting. They were seeing their employees grow in their ability to communicate and their teams working better together. Each training session was positive and affirming. I knew I was in a good place, and I knew that I was working with a good person. I knew that I had become attracted to Tom.

After an extensive training session in Downtown St. Louis, Tom and I stopped at the Galleria Mall for dinner. In the middle of the Galleria was a charming restaurant, surrounded by an indoor pond, complete with goldfish and its own bridge. We ordered dinner, crossed the bridge, and sat down at the café-style tables while waiting for our meal to be served. Fearful of being disappointed again, I wanted to know if my attraction to Tom was mutual. *It's best to find out how he feels before I get too attached to the idea of being attracted to him.*

So, during dinner, I gathered all the courage I could and asked him a question that had been on my heart, "Tom ... do you think we're attracted to each other?"

He looked up at me and hesitated. *Now, what do I do? I just laid all my cards on the table. What if he doesn't feel the way I do? How will I get through this dinner? How will I face him at work tomorrow? But, ... I have to know."*

Tom looked at me in the eyes and smiled, "I can't speak for *you*, but I know *I* am attracted to you..."

I smiled and responded, "...I can speak for me, and I *know* I am attracted to you."

We held hands, and my heart overflowed. The Rendezvous Café became our favorite place to eat. We began spending our weekends together bike riding or rollerblading through Forest Park or walking through the St. Louis Zoo, and hours talking about everything under the sun. Within a year, Tom and I married. We bought a little home nestled on a cul-de-sac in O'Fallon, Missouri, just west of St. Louis, and were excitedly expecting our first child.

I was thirty-six years old and early in our marriage when Tom and I had our first major conflict. I was pregnant and dealing with the unexpected changes that pregnancy brings. I remember feeling vulnerable and completely out of control because my body was doing whatever it wanted. I felt insecure as I witnessed my flat tummy expand and all-too-often hysterical emotional responses to circumstances that would typically have met with some level of self-control. I don't remember what we argued about, I know I felt misunderstood, and that out of frustration, I raised my hand to hit Tom. Mid-air, Tom grabbed my wrist and stopped me. I still did not have the skills to articulate my emotions. I didn't know how to seek to understand another person's perspective in the heat of a battle or help a person understand mine.

I lived in dysfunction most of my life, and anger was the only language I knew how to speak during any intense personal conflict. I was used to being written off, rejected, or pushed around, and as soon as I felt Tom's hand stop my attempt to lash out at him, a sinking feeling hit my heart. *I blew it! I blew the only good thing I had. This is when I exit stage left.*

I expected Tom to respond by saying, "I didn't sign up for this, Mary Ann! You're childish and out of control; I want you to leave, now!" I envisioned packing and wondered where I would go. *Maybe back to Mom's? I can't bear the thought of starting over again.*

Tom stopped me from hitting him, and while he was holding my hand in the air, he calmly looked into my eyes and said, "Mary Ann, we don't do that here."

My eyes met his, and I wasn't able to adequately express what I was feeling, so I simply responded by whispering, "OK." But in my heart, I heard two keywords loud and clear, *we* and *here*. He didn't say *I*, as in, "I don't want you anymore." And he didn't say *there*, as in "You need to leave and go somewhere else." He said *we* and *here*. *We* don't do that *here*. I was no longer just *me*; I was part of a *we*, and I was no longer *there*; I had a *here* to belong to. I was home. And even though Tom and I have experienced our challenges, as all marriages do, that was a defining moment for me. *If he can be that patient with me, then I will learn to be that patient with him, as well.*

LOVE TUGGED ON MY HEART

Tommy arrived on January 18, and we fell in love with him completely. We were totally smitten. His arrival changed the course of our lives. We were a family and so utterly elated. Tommy was the center of our lives, and we were devoted to creating an environment of love and security.

Tom and I attended church together on Sunday mornings. I was surprised by how much I responded to worship. As an adult, the only time I remember singing out loud so passionately was in the shower or while driving alone. The music and the words pierced me to the core. While worshiping God, I often felt a tug on my heart that I didn't understand. *Can a love like this really exist?*

One morning when the pastor shared that God's love is unconditional and that there is nothing we can do to earn it or purchase it, I felt the tug on my heart again. He explained that God gave each person the gift of free will, and each person has used their free will to transgress against God. Instinctively I knew that I have been super selfish and self-centered. *It's true. There is no denying that I made decisions that I knew were wrong.*

The pastor went on to explain that the penalty for our transgressions is separation from God. I felt the weight of my decisions when I went the opposite direction that my conscience was trying to take me.

He continued sharing the gravity of our situation – our wayward hearts have created a chasm that we cannot repair. That chasm has created an emptiness in our hearts that only God can fill. *I have felt that emptiness.*

The pastor stated, "There is only one person who is able to repair the breach, and that is God's Son, Jesus. He is the only person who lived perfectly by loving God and humanity more than wanting to satisfy a selfish desire or rebellious bent."

He further explained, "Jesus became a man and gave His life and His lifeblood as payment for every transgression committed on the earth. He lived the life we should have lived and died the death we deserved. We are required to do one thing, and that is to accept that Jesus did this on our behalf, turn to Him in humility, confess our mistakes, receive His gift of forgiveness, and love Him with all our heart, mind, soul and strength."

The pastor asked if anyone would like to come to the front of the church and accept Jesus' gift of salvation. I walked down the aisle before he finished his sentence. An older lady who wore her grey hair in a bun and a beautiful pink scarf around her neck placed my hands in hers. We prayed together, and while the skies didn't open up and the heavens didn't shake, I felt a peace come over me like a warm blanket. *Thank you, Jesus.*

I wish I could say that everything was OK after that. You would think that having every mistake wiped clean and starting a clean slate would be enough, but I struggled.

A VOICE FROM THE PAST

I couldn't get Helen out of my mind. It had been over ten years since we talked. We didn't have the internet then to help us search for people, and the number I had was no longer hers. After many failed attempts to reach her, I remembered that her brother-in-law owned a real estate agency. Sure enough, he still did. He remembered me, gave me her number, and I called Helen. Her voice hadn't changed, always joyful.

"Helen, this is Mary Ann Huber, now Otley. Do you remember me?"

"Mary Ann, how are you? Of course, I remember you," she exclaimed with excitement.

"I'm well, Helen. Some things have transpired in my life, and I just had to find you and tell you."

"Well, tell me, I'm on pins and needles?"

After all these years, she hadn't changed a bit, still purely delightful.

"Helen, I accepted Jesus as my Lord and my Savior, and I just had to find you and tell you."

There was silence on the phone.

"Helen, are you there?"

"Yes," she answered, "I am," her voice cracked. "Mary Ann, this means so much to me personally that you would call and let me tell you why. For years, and I mean years, the Lord would wake me up at 4 a.m., and tell me, 'Get on your knees, Mary Ann needs prayer.'"

Tears welled up in my eyes, and I had a knowing in my heart that her prayers, her obedience, and her relationship with God helped me through the toughest of times.

"Helen, there were times when I would think, 'How did I escape death?' or 'How did I stop drinking and snorting cocaine? How did that happen?' and I have to believe that in the midst of my mess, Jesus loved me all along and gave me beautiful gifts like you."

We lived miles away from each other and vowed to stay in touch, exchanged Christmas Cards, and when Facebook came into being, she was one of my first Facebook friends. And sure enough, faithfully, Helen posts a scripture each day, and each day I read it and "love" it. Helen's acceptance of me was comforting. *How could she be so loving? I had rejected her! I chose Mr. High Society instead of her and Jesus.*

My heart felt light after talking with Helen. Her intercession had been an unseen source of strength for me for years prior, and now it would be a consistent source of strength as our relationship as sisters in faith grew.

JESUS SWINGS WITH CHILDREN

I was thirty-nine years old and still had layers of unresolved pain, shame, disappointment, discouragement, and fear. My faith in Jesus as God still wavered. I had developed more respect for Jesus, but *What if the pastor is wrong? What if it was just an emotional response I had? What if I heard what I wanted to hear? How can I know for sure that this is true?*

I would worship Jesus on Sunday and by Wednesday dismiss Him as God and rationalize that he was an exceptional person that made history. This waffling was a pattern that went on for a couple of years. When I was at church, I believed. When I was at home, I questioned.

The uncertainty was getting to me. I hate it when things are unresolved. *What if I am playing the fool again? What if all this is nonsense? What if this whole Jesus thing is just a way for someone to make money? What if I believe that Jesus is God, then I die, face God, and find out that this is all a lie.*

I can just imagine God saying, "Mary Ann, you are a fool. You believed that a MAN could be God?!" With thunderbolts and lightning flashing all around me, God would pronounce. "I hereby sentence you to Hell for eternity for being so stupid!"

Finally, on a sunny afternoon, while our son, Tommy, was napping, I finished the breakfast dishes. My thoughts were screaming to God; *I can't take going back and forth any longer. I need to know one way or another. Can we just settle this? I have been wrong about so many things. How do I know if this is right? If you're God, then you could tell me! If you're God, you could resolve this once and for all!* The battle in my mind caused turmoil and uncertainty. I just wanted to know.

God, I am told that all I have to do is trust you. How is that fair? You've got this backward. I feel I am being set up to fail. I mean, I trusted Dad, I trusted the Dentist, I trusted what appeared to be a Good Samaritan. Look what happened! If I need to trust you, then I need you to help me. If You are God, and you want me to believe that Jesus is your Son and he also is God, then you are going to have to tell me. Then I'll believe you and trust you.

Tommy, not even three years old at the time, had woken up from his nap, walked down the stairs over to me, and began tugging on my pant leg, "Mommy, Mommy."

"Yes, Tommy," I answered a tad bit abruptly because I *was* in the middle of a silent but intense, one-way rant with God.

Tommy looked up at me with great anticipation, "Mommy, Jesus is God!"

What?! I turned and squatted to face him eye-to-eye and asked him to repeat what he said, "Tommy, honey, what did you just say?"

Innocently, he repeated himself, "Mommy, Jesus is God."

I couldn't believe my ears. I had never prayed a word out loud. They were silent pleadings… well, more like demands. I gazed at Tommy, who looked as if he held a secret treasure; I brushed his blonde hair back away from his beautiful, sleepy, green eyes and asked, "Tommy, what makes you say that?"

He looked at me matter-of-factly and said, "We were swinging together, Mommy. Jesus and I were swinging." Tommy continued, "Our swings were connected and the swings went all the way up to the sky, and God's angels were all around us." *What? How can this be?*

"And, Mommy, the Holy Spirit pushed us!"

I knelt in disbelief. At first, I tried to understand logically how he could have been swinging with anyone and wondered how Tommy could know about the Holy Spirit. It was a miracle!

But hope filled my heart, and a question came to my mind, "Tommy, what did Jesus *look* like?!"

Tommy looked at me wide-eyed and said, "Mommy, He looks like a light. Jesus is a light."

"Did He speak to you, Tommy?"

"No, Mommy. We just laughed," and Tommy added, "Mommy, I didn't want him to go."

"Sweetheart, what happened next?" I asked. He answered simply, "I woke up."

The reality was overwhelming. While I was grappling with God, He gave Tommy a beautiful experience to answer the cries of my heart. Tommy was able to articulate concepts far beyond his age. I hugged and kissed Tommy. After I made him a snack, I retrieved a journal I kept to record Tommy's special moments and wrote every word to commemorate this day.

On this day, the God, that I was so afraid of believing in, visited my son. He sent Tommy as a messenger to settle the matter. Jesus is God. Jesus is a light. Jesus laughs and swings with children. Jesus is accompanied by angels and the Holy Spirit.

As a firstborn, Tommy was used to all of our attention. Rarely did he stay with a babysitter without crying for us; yet, Jesus made Tommy feel safe, so safe, that Tommy didn't want him to leave. I wanted to experience Jesus for myself. I wanted to know the God that swings and laughs with children.

Every night, before I fell asleep, I begged God, "Would You come to visit me like You visited Tommy. Please God, visit me like You visited Tommy. I must experience You for myself." I was relentless in my prayers and determined to continually ask Him until He came. And then one night, He did.

Jesus came to me in a dream. The dream felt as real as rain, and in it, I was attending a bible study. The room was full of women. We faced the front of the room and were intently listening to our teacher. Spontaneously, there was an awareness among the women. Everyone understood that something had happened, everyone but me. I saw each woman stand and then turn to face the back of the room. I stood up as I watched each woman fall to her knees in adoration. *What could impact them so profoundly?*

Out of curiosity, I turned to the back of the room, and that is when I saw Him. It was Jesus. He had entered in the back door, and while each woman knelt in reverence and respect for Him, He waited … for me.

His eyes met mine. He was dressed in white, and He gleamed dazzlingly. He was beautiful. Tommy's description was accurate. He is a man, and He is a brilliant light. *There is no darkness in Him.* I was aware that, except for Jesus, I was the only one in the room standing. I felt uncomfortable about that. *Why did I not bow or kneel? Why am I the only one standing? How did they know to bow?*

Unexpectedly, a prayer I had learned as a little girl emerged from my heart and out of my lips, and I spoke to Him, "Lord, I am not worthy to receive you. But, only say the word, and my soul will be healed." My heart was pounding.

As He looked at me, I was aware of my need for Him. He didn't acknowledge my neediness, my weakness, nor my sin(s), but looked at me and kindly Jesus spoke these simple words of instruction, "Be humble."

The dream ended as soon as it appeared.

I understood what Tommy meant when he said, "Mommy, I didn't want him to go."

I sat up. *Oh my God! Jesus just came to me! He spoke to me!* Then I remembered his words, *Be humble. Humble? I'm not sure I even know what that means. I have to find out.* I leaned over to turn on my bedside lamp and jumped out of bed to retrieve our dictionary, which was on the bookshelf just three feet from me. I brought the dictionary back to bed and quickly searched it to find the true meaning of humility.

Thumbing through, I found the word humility.

Humility. A noun.
Meekness.
What!? Isn't meekness weakness? Why would I want to be meek!

An additional word followed, Modesty. *Modest? Another word I would have to look up.* More definitions of humility followed: A low view of one's own importance. *A low view? Are you serious? That's what I have been trying to escape all my life.*

I continued to read from the page: lack of vanity, submissiveness. *Submissiveness, why would He want me to be submissive! Isn't that a bit archaic?*

Antonyms: pride. *Isn't pride good? Aren't we supposed to want to be on the top, not on the bottom?*

"Jesus, can You give me another assignment? Please."

LEARNING FROM CHILDREN

Tom's mother had passed away during Tommy's second year of life. She was a blessing, and it was a difficult time. She had given Tom and me many books to read to Tommy, including a set of bible stories for children. I had not valued them, chocked them off as the token child gift, and they sat on the bookshelf until now. I wanted to know more about Tommy's Jesus. I had never read a bible, so together, Tommy and I were introduced to the life stories of Noah and the Ark, Moses and the Israelites, David and Goliath, Jonah and the Whale, Elijah and Baal's prophets, Jesus and His disciples, and Jesus and His miracles. It was another real beginning that led me to understand better the questions I had asked earlier in my life. What is real? What is important? What is the truth?

At thirty-nine years old, we were expecting our second child. Once Johnny arrived, Tommy asked incessantly, "Daddy, when do I get to *wrestle* him?"

"It will be a little while," Tom explained, "For now, Johnny needs you to hold him and protect him." With a new-found sense of responsibility, Tommy took being a big brother seriously. He meticulously checked everyone's hands before they touched Johnny, being sure each hand had been properly washed. Tommy stood guard as the neighborhood kids came to hold Johnny. He took naps with him, fed him his first spoonful of real food, and patiently helped Johnny speak his first word, "bubby" for puppy. They were inseparable. And in due time, Johnny grew old enough to where they wrestled to their heart's content.

I was invited to a Bible Study by Terri, a wonderfully kind lady who watched Tommy while I worked part-time. I was nervous because I knew no one at the Bible Study, nor had I ever attended a Bible Study, but I had promised Terri I would visit at least once. They were studying the Book of John. I found my place amidst a room of approximately 50 women. Roma, the teacher, was in the front of the room and explained that the Book of John is about the extravagant love that God has for each and every one of us.

She explained that as we know Jesus and love Jesus, mysteries are revealed, and we experience His beauty and glory. As we know and experience Jesus' love, we stop defining ourselves by our successes and failures but by His love and as one of His dearly loved children. As the words filled the room, I felt a rush of wind blow right through me, literally. It was comforting. I wanted to grab it, bottle it, and hold on to it. I looked around the room. It was a crisp, cool Fall day. There were no fans running, no windows opened. *Where did that wind come from?*

As I returned to the Bible Study in the following weeks, there were times I could feel that soft breeze hover over me. Peace. I would later learn that what I was experiencing was a manifestation of God's presence through His Spirit. After that experience, I committed to being there every week. And while I was there, while we were studying the Book of John and sharing the revelation we received while doing our homework, I saw a vision of Jesus.

While the Bible study was going on around me, everything seemed to stop for just a brief moment, and before me, I saw a dirt road and sandaled feet walking down a dusty path. It was profound. The reality that those were "His" sandals and "His" feet was absolute.

I responded by whispering, "Jesus, you were really here, weren't you? You became a man, and you walked these dusty roads to help us, didn't you?"

I felt that He shared a treasure with me in a very personal way. Even though it was only a vision of His sandaled feet, I felt His personality, faithfulness, strength, steadfastness, and love. I fell in love with those feet and the character of the man they belonged to. I whispered, "Jesus, I love you."

My faith in Jesus was still very new. There was so much to learn, and so many of the women around me appeared to be very knowledgeable about Him. I still had many ideas and misperceptions about God, life, and death that I learned from all the searching I had done in the past. But God was faithful and patient with me.

A LESSON IN TRUTH

With my child abuse background, Tom and I took every precaution to ensure that our children would not be left in a vulnerable situation or alone with people we did not know. Even in Church. Tommy attended Children's Church, and I attended with him. Tommy and the other children sat in a circle around Miss Nikki, the bible teacher. Johnny, still very young, sat in my lap at the back of the room watching.

Miss Nikki began to ask the children questions, "So, I have a question for all of you, if someone goes to church *every* Sunday and *never* misses, will they go to Heaven?"

Sure, I answered silently to myself.

"NO!" shouted the kids emphatically.

What? Why wouldn't they? Wouldn't you love God if you went to church every Sunday? I was puzzled.

Nikki responded to the kids, "That's exactly right; we don't *earn* our way to Heaven."

She asked another question, "So, how *do* we get into heaven?

"Jesus is the way," yelled a little girl with big blue eyes and flaming red hair that was braided in pigtails.

I better pay attention, I thought protectively; I *don't want Tommy to be brainwashed.*

"OK, I have another question for you," said Nikki. I moved in closer.

"What if you are *really, really, really* good? Can you go to heaven?"

Well, sure. What's the point of being good if you don't go to heaven?

"NO!" screamed the kids.

A little boy with deep brown eyes and an engaging smile confidently declared, "Church is where we meet to worship Jesus, but being good or going to church does not mean we go to heaven."

"That's right, Cameron! We don't go to Heaven based on our good deeds. We go to Heaven based upon what Jesus accomplished for us on the Cross. He made the way for us." Miss Nikki responded.

Nikki continued, "Now, another question, "What if you gave *everything* you owned to help the poor? Would you be *guaranteed* to go to heaven and live with Jesus?"

Of course. I mean, you just gave everything! I reasoned.

A little girl with blonde banana curls waved her hand furiously. She began bouncing up and down, trying to get Nikki's attention, "I know the answer to that one. I know the answer!"

Oh my goodness, *for God's sakes, answer her. I've got to know!*

"Wonderful, Julie! What is your answer?"

87

Julie stood up confidently and recited, "If I give ALL my money to the poor and have not LOVE, it counts for nothing!"

Doesn't it take love to do something that extravagant? I questioned myself.

"Thank you, Susie. There are people in the world that do good deeds because they want *praise* from other people; we all want to stay away from that."

Nikki added, "And also, some people believe that they can *buy* their way into heaven by doing extravagant deeds for God. But God doesn't look at the outward appearance and actions of people; God looks at our hearts. What kind of heart does God ask us to have?"

"Obedient" came a voice from a little boy with jet black hair and big, round brown eyes who responded without taking his eyes off the little, red fire truck he drove in circles, carefully driving inside the patterns on the carpet in front of him.

Nikki answered him, "Obedience is important, Ben, but what do you need to be in order to be obedient?"

"Loving," whispered a little girl with adorable freckles, dressed in a green plaid dress and sporting new, pink princess shoes.

Nikki responded, "Being loving is also very important. But I'm looking for a certain word. I'll give you a hint. You fill in the blank. Moses was able to talk to God face-to-face because Moses was _____?"

Silence.

My face grew flush and hot; Here I am, in a room full of four and five-year old's and felt as intimidated as if I were speaking to a room full of Harvard professors. I had just read to Tommy from his collection of bible stories that Moses was the humblest man in all the world. Truthfully, at the time I read it, I wasn't impressed; I still didn't see humility as a particularly valuable attribute.

"Humble?" I asked Nikki shyly from the back of the room.

"Yes! Mrs. Otley! Thank you!"

Well, there is hope for me after all. Put a gold sticker on my forehead.

Nikki continued, "God asks us to have a humble heart. Being humble means that we don't puff ourselves up or consider that we are better than others. If we did puff ourselves up and try to be better than others, that would be being proud, and when we're proud, we don't love well.

So that's why Jesus wants me to be humble.

"We want to be humble, so our hearts are positioned right to love God well and love others well," Nikki concluded, "Let's bow our heads and pray that God would help each one of us be humble this week." Heads bowed, hands locked with fingers crossed, little voices whispered their simple requests to God.

I couldn't hold back the tears as I was convicted of my arrogance. For most of my adult life, I lived in circles where Jesus wasn't fashionable and often unacceptable.

I whispered to myself, "I used to make fun of this."

I was the first to tell the latest 'Jesus' joke. I believed that Jesus was for the weak, the losers.

I bowed my head with the four and five-year old's and asked God to have mercy upon me and teach me to be humble.

WHAT DOES IT MEAN TO LIVE A GODLY LIFE

After that experience, I pondered, "what does it mean to truly follow God and live a Godly life?"

I believe God heard my thoughts that day and answered them. While dusting, a book my sister-in-law Mary gave to me seemed to hop off the shelf. I opened The Power of a Pray Wife by Stormie Omartian and found a distant companion. Stormy became my tutor. As I read through each chapter and prayed each prayer for Tom, God began to teach me about His character. I was introduced to Biblical principles like truth, transparency, confession, repentance, and forgiveness. In her books, Stormie shares her own story of experiencing childhood trauma and how turning to Jesus in her young adult years was the key to living a life of peace and joy. Each chapter ends with a scriptural prayer asking God to bring His truth and goodness into our lives. While being introduced to the goodness of God, I still secretly believed that God the Father was holding a hammer just waiting to crush me for my transgressions. Yet, I could feel the power of praying Biblical prayers. I was learning more about God.

HE SEES BEYOND MY MESS

At age forty-one, and with our third child on the way, the lack of sleep and toddlers' demands was taking its toll on me. Tom's responsibilities required him to travel more and more. I was no longer attending adult church but was teaching Tommy and Johnny's children's Sunday School.

I felt distant from God and wanted to experience Jesus again. Thoughts of condemnation kept creeping in my mind. While lying in bed one night, I begged him to help me.

"I feel I'm slipping away from you, Jesus. I'm full of unbelief again. I've made so many mistakes in my life. I can't bear to make

90

any more. Please don't be angry with me. Please reveal the truth to me again," I prayed.

I still had so many unresolved wounds from my past. And even though I was teaching Children's Sunday School, I had lost sight of the simple truth, that His arms were open, and His heart was full of love for me. I waited to hear from Him, and He answered me. With my eyes closed in prayer, I saw Him.

He was so close I could almost feel His breath, and he spoke to me, "Let Me in."

As soon as my answer, "But I already have let you in," rolled off my tongue, I was aware that I had invited Jesus into my mind, my thoughts, my reason, but had not asked him into the private and remote places of my heart.

"I can't," I whispered to Him. Thinking of the depths of darkness hidden in the secret places of my heart, I whispered to Him. "I have to clean it first."

He replied to me, "That's not possible, not without Me."

I was in a dilemma.

Fear struck my heart for Him. He is so pure, so good, so true, so kind.

I became worried for His welfare and pleaded, "I can't let you in. It's dark in here. Roaches live in there. It's too painful to think about. People get hurt in there. And, if you enter into my heart, I'm not sure you will come out the same; I don't know if you will survive it. I cannot allow you in here."

Jesus reassured me, "I know what is in there, and I won't get hurt. Trust Me. Letting Me in is the only way."

And then I confided to him and whispered, "I don't know how."

Then, He was gone.

When He was no longer in front of me, I assumed He was gone. But when I closed my eyes in prayer, I found myself standing in a prison cell. The dark place within me that I didn't want him to enter, I was now in. There was no life in it and no doors. The despair was so thick I could hardly breathe. I looked around; it was dreary and empty. It is a gloomy place where guilt, condemnation, and shame go in, but they don't go out. I began to feel the despair that I had tried to run from most of my life, the looming questions of my past, *Where do I belong? How will I ever fit in? Why am I bad? How do I escape the pain?*

My heart was sinking in despair when I noticed a small window positioned at the top of the cell. Light was peering through it, and I followed the light to the floor of the prison cell … and that is when I saw Him. Dressed in a white robe with a sash around his waist, Jesus was kneeling on the floor, humble and radiant. He had a scrub brush in one hand and a bucket on the floor beside Him. He was not influenced by the darkness; it couldn't touch Him. He dipped the brush into the bucket and began to clean the floor of my heart. Every place He touched turned to brilliant light. As Jesus scrubbed, the dark cell transformed into a place filled with light. Roaches were gone. Grime was gone. Darkness was gone. Bright light flooded my spirit as peace wrapped around my mind and heart like a blanket.

For the first time in my life, I felt God knew I truly existed. I felt "seen." Jesus saw me beyond the dirt, the grime, the guilt, the fear, and the shame I felt. He wasn't looking at my failures. I did not offend him, and my past did not distract him from loving me. I spent years of my life looking for value, significance, purpose, and safety. And in one night, in one instance, He revealed to me the truth of my identity; that I was valuable enough for Him to break into that prison; and that I was significant enough for Him to clean my heart. My purpose was to know Him more and be like Him. And I felt completely safe in His presence.

At the same time, He taught me that many of my beliefs about Him were not true. He wasn't trying to make me follow an impossible set of rules. He wasn't disappointed in me. He didn't yell, ridicule, or preach at me. He simply washed all of the toxicity away. His light overcame the darkness I harbored, and His love overcame my fears. I felt found, and I felt loved. His loving and powerful actions created a desire to want to know Him more, and for the first time, I trusted God. I wanted to follow Him and trusted that any design He has for me and my life would be for my good.

The Creator of the Universe showed me the beauty of humility. *Oh, how I want to be like you. Oh, how I want to be humble.*

I peacefully drifted to sleep.

HE CALLS US BY NAME

Tom was at a point in his career where he was traveling a great deal. At times, he would be out of the Country for a week, come home for a quick weekend, and need to fly out again on Monday. With three children under ten years old, we found creative ways to cope. We put an iPad at the head of the table and had dinner with Daddy virtually. We made surprises, home-made gifts, and home videos to give him upon his return. But the traveling took its toll on everyone. The kids were missing him, and I was weary from parenting without a break.

One Sunday evening, we tearfully drove away from St. Louis Airport as Tom boarded a flight to China. We headed back home for a movie night to curb the disappointment. As I accelerated and entered traffic on Interstate 70, emotions accelerated in the back of the van. Questions were tearfully filling the air.

93

"Mommy, why don't you let Daddy stay home?!"

"Mommy, why does Daddy always have to go on a business trip? Why don't you go?!"

How do I explain to a seven-year-old that sees me make decisions that affect every part of his life, every day, that I am not the boss of <u>everything</u>?

Things didn't get better when we got home. There were full-blown temper tantrums, and I finally put everyone to bed early - with no movie. *I've had it. I can't do this anymore. I am exhausted and wish I could fly away somewhere.*

Finally, when everyone was sleeping and the house grew quiet, I climbed the stairs and started my bedtime routine. While I brushed my teeth, I had a private, nonverbal rant with God. You know, the kind of private tirade where your mind spins in circles with thoughts you think but never dare say out loud for fear of looking like an utter mess.

Do you see how everyone treats me? Do you see how I am here every morning, every day, and every night? But they want Tom more than me! (Tears) *Do you see me wiping mouths, wiping noses, wiping bottoms, and wiping floors day in and day out? Who is taking care of every detail? Me! Who is driving them to and fro and to and fro — day in and day out? Me! Who reads to them, does their lesson plans, teaches them? Me! Tom is flying to China where he will eat authentic Chinese while I stay at home eating Cheerios and Macaroni and Cheese? I didn't sign up for this!! What's my purpose? Am I completely forgotten and unimportant, a nobody? No one sees me. What about me, God?* I wasn't expecting an answer, but I got one.

With my mouth filled with toothpaste and my heart filled with fury, I looked in the mirror feeling hopelessly pathetic.

And God spoke to me, "Tommy's name is Beautiful."

94

I spit the toothpaste from my mouth.

He spoke again, "Johnny's name is Precious."

I dropped my toothbrush.

"And Iris," He said affectionately, "Iris' name is Wonderful."

I dropped to my knees, convicted of my attitude, and cried. "Please forgive me. I forgot what this is all about."

I climbed into bed and carried the beauty of God's still small (yet powerful) voice. I was in awe of His character; there was no condemnation. He didn't correct me sternly, nor did He appear to be angry, discouraged, or disappointed in me.

He had every right to respond with a sharp rebuke, "Listen, young lady! You have a job to do, and you need to get with the program!"

But, no, He taught me about my children's identity. *My children are not 'work'; they are Beautiful, Precious, and Wonderful. My kids are valuable to God — so much so that He has unique names for each of them. That's remarkable.*

While I was complaining about parenting, He was parenting me. I fell asleep with a wave of peace over my heart that only a Father God could produce.

The next morning, I jumped out of bed and made the kids' breakfast. We sat around the table, and I shared with them what God spoke to me the night before.

"Mommy was mad last night. And I am very sorry for being angry with you. I told God that I was angry, and He told me something very, very important. He told me you each have a unique Name that He calls you. Special names just for you!"

Their eyes looked at me intently, waiting to hear their names.

"Tommy, God said your name is Beautiful."

Tommy smiled.

"Johnny, He said your name is Precious."

Johnny smiled.

Iris, God calls you Wonderful."

Iris giggled.

When he looks down from heaven and looks at you, that's how He sees you."

I don't know how I expected them to respond, but their response caught me off guard.

Tommy and Johnny looked at me with serious expressions on their faces and simultaneously they asked, "What's Daddy's name?"

What!? What's Daddy's name? Who am I? Chopped liver? I'll tell you what Daddy's name is ... Let's start with 'Absent!'

I curbed my offended heart, redirected my insulting thoughts, and replied, "Let's ask Jesus."

Tommy and Johnny closed their eyes, folded their hands, and asked, "Jesus, what is Daddy's name?"

I was still feeling the offense of parenting and home educating alone while my husband soars in his career. Their gleeful answer interrupted my thoughts by simultaneously blurting out with tremendous pride, "Daddy's name is Great!"

There was so much excitement in their eyes. And again, there was that resoluteness in their voices – much like I heard the night before.

Great!? Wait. Let me think. What does great mean, biblically? I was convicted - my heart and attitude were not even close to God's. *What's wrong with me? Why am I so angry with Tom? Why wouldn't "Great" be great with me?*

It hit me, "Kids, do you know what the word great means to God?"

"No, Mommy," they thoughtfully answered.

"The person that is called 'great' in God's Kingdom is a faithful servant," I replied as I reflected on the kind of work my husband does. "Daddy serves people by helping them be good leaders. Good leaders help other people be happy in their work and their families. Daddy has a very good heart, and he loves serving God and people." I replied.

My heart softened toward Tom. *He is great, isn't he, Lord?*

Tom knows no stranger, and he invests himself in any person that is put in his path. It didn't matter who the person was, what their station in life was, or how they looked; Tom invested himself in each person to help them reach a better quality of life. While my ideas were soaked in self-pity and my perspective of my family was 180 degrees from God's, God kindly pointed me in the right direction, and He reset my compass to true North.

After the kids finished their breakfast and began to get ready for school, I returned to the bathroom floor and knelt at the same place God met me the night before, "Lord, I have believed lies about the most valuable people in my life. Please forgive me."

I didn't feel like I deserved my own name from God, and at the same time, I didn't want to go on without one. "Lord, what's *my* name?" I asked.

I heard an instant response in the center of my being, "You are Mine." I felt the letters M-I-N-E inscribed inside of me. Amid my complaining and self-pity, God spoke to me about my identity. *I am His. I am Yours. What else matters?*

I knelt on the bathroom floor for a while until the sacred moment was interrupted by calls from my children downstairs, "Mommy, we need you!"

I tucked the moment into my heart and happily wiped the tears from my eyes, and responded, "I'm on my way!"

HE CAUSES HORNETS TO FLEE

At forty-six years old, we were still living in our home in O'Fallon, MO and our lives were busier than ever.

Jesus had indeed entered into my spirit and made me His. I treasured the memory of Him entering into the secret places of my heart. His light is living within me. I thought that would mean all is good now. But there were more emotions and memories from my past I had not yet dealt with. The unresolved issues of being sexually abused and raped began manifesting, often in the middle of the night.

"Why did you touch me like that?" I tersely responded to Tom's advance.

"Like what?" he asked.

"You know, like *that!*" I said with anger in my voice.

"I don't know what you are referring to, Mary Ann."

"Tom, how could you be so insensitive?!" I replied.

"What did I do?" he asked, confused.

"Seriously!?" I responded indignantly.

"Seriously, what?" he responded.

"You touched me THERE (pointing to a part of my body) and in the middle of the night!" I said accusingly.

"So?!" he responded.

"So?! How could you?!!" I answered indignantly.

"How could I what? I LOVE you! I love touching you. You're my wife!" Tom explained, bewildered.

"If you LOVED me, you would know better than to ..."

"Know better than TO what?!" he asked.

"Touch me *there*!" I screamed.

"Mary Ann, I am your husband! I want to touch you everywhere!" he continued.

"Men! That's all they think about!"

"What! You know that's not true. Let me run you a bath. You've been taking care of everyone, and you're just exhausted," he reasoned.

"Oh great! Just get me in a bath, in the middle of the night, NAKED, and all will be OK! I'm not falling for that one!"

Anger filled my heart as a great distance and divide began to emerge inside of me toward Tom. He responded,

"Honey, when I'm gone, all I do is think about you. I love you!"

"Well, all I think about is my pillow! All I want is to go somewhere quiet and sleep." I answered, then I broke down. "Tom, something's wrong with me. While I'm awake, all I can think of is when I will sleep again. I'm irritable all the time. I'm exhausted. I'm a mess."

The fatigue I was experiencing frightened me, and then it all began to unravel one day after Tom left for New York on business. I was forty-seven years old. Tommy was ten, Johnny was eight, and Iris was five. We were still in the little house we bought when we were first married. It was a beautiful sunny day, and the kids played in the backyard all morning. I prepared lunch, and when they came in hungry, I told Tommy, "Mommy is going to take a 10-minute nap while you eat. Would you please keep an eye on Johnny and Iris for me?" I flopped onto the couch, wrapped myself in a blanket, and didn't wake up until 10 hours later. The kids were scared when they couldn't wake me up, and Tommy called Tom. Tom called a friend to look after the kids. He took the next flight home.

From that day and for months to follow, I slept 20 hours a day, only to wake up feeling exhausted. I never felt refreshed. Because I could not care for Tommy, Johnny, and Iris, Tom took the kids to work with him until a person at his office complained. After that, friends from church volunteered to pick up Tommy, Johnny, and Iris in the morning and bring them back in the evening with a delicious, home-made dinner. Of all my life's memories, this is still the most difficult to remember – day after day, someone else was caring for my family ... while I slept.

Earlier that year, I had completed a bible study by Henry Blackaby called, Experiencing God. In it, he explains that God is always speaking to us and explains how we can hear God, sense His leading, and join Him in His purposes. That study proved to be providential to me. With Tom at work and the kids at a friend's home, my growling stomach would wake me up in the afternoon. I struggled to walk downstairs to get something to eat and read my bible. By this time, every step was painful. I felt like I was going crazy. A burning sensation would appear in my neck; the next day, it would be in my knees and the next my back. Arthritis appeared in my wrists and hands. Walking was painful, and even though I was only in my forties, I was bent over like a little old lady.

I couldn't think clearly. One day while Tom was out of town, I tried to drive to the grocery store, which was a little over a mile away, and I got lost. One Saturday morning, the kids asked me to make their favorite breakfast, French toast, but I could not gather my thoughts enough to remember how to do it. One thing that I was able to do was read my bible. And each day, as I ate lunch alone, I read it, and each day a verse would stand out just like Henry Blackaby said it would, almost declaring, "Pay attention to this!" As a verse jumped off the page, I recorded it onto a sheet of copy paper with a black Sharpie and then taped it to the kitchen wall.

Eventually, my kitchen was wall-papered with Bible verses like:

"Not by might, nor by power, but by my spirit." Zechariah 4:6

"I am the Lord, and there is no one else. There is no savior besides me." Isaiah 45:5-6

"Love the Lord your God with all your heart, and all your soul and all your mind, and with all your strength." Matt 12:30

"As the Father has loved Me, so also have I loved you; remain in My love." John 15:9

"Call upon Me on the day of trouble; I will rescue you, and you will honor Me." Psalm 50:15

"Do not fear or be dismayed because of this great multitude, for the battle is not yours but God's." 2 Chronicles 20:15

Tom and I visited doctor after doctor, and no one could determine what was wrong with me. I explained that my neck ached, then my side, then my ankles and wrists. At night, the pain was so excruciating that I would bite my blanket to get relief – I bit that blanket so hard that I created TMJ that would later require braces to eliminate the neck strain and headaches. We sought several doctors and walked out of their offices with various anti-depressant prescriptions in hand and the same diagnosis, depression.

I told each doctor, "Please listen; I'm not depressed. I'm tired!"

Doctors didn't know how to help.

"We need to understand this before we start treating it," Tom said, concerned.

Tom and I agreed that I would not fill the prescriptions until we found the root cause. I moaned, groaned, and slept around the clock. I began sleeping in Iris' room so that I wouldn't disrupt Tom's sleep.

The same day that I had whispered to myself, "I'm dying," Tom came home at lunchtime to check in on me.

"Mary Ann, it smells like a nursing home in here!" he said as he approached me and sat on the bed next to me.

I confessed, "I know. It feels like I'm dying."

He held my hands, got on his knees, and prayed, "Lord, we don't know what to do, Lord, we need your help."

Tom brought me a bowl of tomato soup and returned to work.

102

After he left, I knelt and prayed, "Lord, if I die, please give Tom a wife that loves him and honors him and help her to love my children as if they were her own."

Later that week, Tom and I went to our pastor and discussed my situation with him and his wife. After about 15 minutes into the conversation, Pastor David asked me a question, "Mary Ann, are you angry?"

His question was as if someone turned on the lights for me.

Anger? No one had ever asked me that question. *Yes, I am angry; but there was one problem. I equated anger as the antithesis of nice, and my entire identity still revolved around being nice. So, if I'm angry, I'm sure I'm doing something wrong, and if I'm doing something wrong, I'm going to lose ... I'm not sure what I'll lose ... but I know that anytime I've ever expressed anger, it came at a great cost.*

I was in a room with Tom, the Pastor, and his wife, three people that I trusted, and I gathered the courage to answer his question directly, "Yes. I'm angry. I'm really angry!"

"Are you angry about something or are you angry with someone?" he continued.

"I'm angry at everyone."

"Do you know why?" he asked.

"No," I answered, "I just keep it bottled up," I whispered.

"Why do you feel that way?" he asked.

"Because that is what has always happened in the past. I tell someone I'm angry, they get mad at me. We fight, and someone loses. It's just better to keep it inside," I reasoned.

"You know, I think it would be good if you had prayer," the pastor shared.

Prayer? What good is that going to do?

"There is a group of women who meet here every Wednesday morning. If you would come on Wednesdays, I will ask them to pray over you," he added. *Would prayer stop me from being angry?*

"Let's do this for a few weeks," Pastor David suggested.

Prayer was a mystery to me. When spending the night with my grandparents, I saw my grandfather pray every morning before he left his bathroom. He knelt on the hard floor, kneeling at the bathroom sink, and prayed an entire rosary before he started each day. He struggled with alcohol, and I had heard stories of his rage and anger when he drank. *I wonder if anger is the reason why Grandpa prayed?*

I met weekly with the women, and they prayed with me for at least thirty minutes each time. We met in a small conference room around a table. During our prayer times, we would start with a Bible verse.

Each woman would say a verse out loud, "The Lord is my shepherd."

Then another, "I shall not want."

And then another, "He makes my lie down in green pastures," and yet another, "He restores my soul."

As they gently and reverently spoke these words out loud, peace would enter the room like a gentle cloud. I had never prayed out loud or heard anyone pray out loud outside of a church service. Something inside of me responded, like lit up, when I heard the Bible verses gently spoken.

104

Jackie, the associate pastor's wife, prayed from 2 Chronicles 16:9 from the Bible, "For the eyes of the Lord are searching throughout the earth to show Himself strong for those whose hearts are completely His." I heard her pray, "Father, Mary Ann is depending upon you to search for her, see that her heart is completely yours and she needs you to show yourself strong and help her through the *battle* she is facing."

Her words comforted me. I felt understood. And wondered *A battle? Am I in a battle? Yes, but with who?*

Then another woman would pray from Psalm 34:18, "The Lord is close to the brokenhearted and saves those who are crushed in spirit. Father, you promise that you are close to those who have experienced things in their life that have left them brokenhearted and crushed in spirit." Help Mary Ann know that you are close to her right now."

Again, I felt understood. There was no condemnation as they spoke to God on my behalf. My body began to shake; tears streamed down my eyes. *That is why I am angry. I am crushed, and I don't know how to get un-crushed. I'm a ball of anger.*

They responded to my crying by gently placing their hands on me. One woman placed her hand on my shoulder; I felt a hand on my back, another on my other shoulder, and another on my head. Gentle, loving touches, and each prayed silently as I wept and wept and wept. They were patient and gave me time to cry it out, handing me tissues and whispered prayers of intercession. Once I stopped crying, one woman asked me if I wanted to talk. I looked at their faces. They were sympathetic and loving.

"I felt something come over me," I shared.

"That was the Holy Spirit," one woman whispered kindly.

It felt like the Holy Spirit was rearranging furniture in my heart and mind. I instantly became aware of things that I needed to stop, like, lying and being impatient with the kids. Even taking an extra $10 from the grocery money without talking to Tom about it.

As I spoke the words to them, I felt God take away the burden of carrying them. I no longer had a desire to lie or yell at that the kids or not trust God to provide what I need, even $10. Yet, I felt embarrassed by being so transparent about my behavior and shared how vulnerable I felt.

Kathy, one of the ladies who had been quietly praying throughout our prayer time, spoke up, "Mary Ann, we all stray from God's design for our lives. And God promises that when we return to Him and freely admit it, He is faithful to forgive us and restore us. He promises to cleanse us from that unrighteousness. It feels unnatural to admit our faults publicly, yet it is the very path we need to walk to be restored."

Her gentle words of wisdom were comforting to me. She not only helped me understand, but I felt God was using her to restore my dignity as well.

She added, "Mary Ann, God encourages us to acknowledge how we have offended each other, and then pray for one another to be instantly healed. God's power to heal is often found in confession and forgiveness. What you have demonstrated is humility, and God is responding to your humility by removing your offense and healing you." *Wow. This is humility. I would have never guessed it took so much courage to be humble. And I had never considered that God had instructed me to "be humble," so I could experience his forgiveness and love.*

I was overwhelmed by God's love and by his kindness through these women.

They were all busy mothers, and I thanked them for taking time out of their week to pray for me.

One woman sat next to me and shared that the reason they pray is not just for other people, but for themselves too, as well, "Mary Ann, we are all on a journey to deeper healing. We need this prayer time just as much as you do. We come together because we know where our healing comes from; it comes from Him alone."

She shared with me that she had experienced a very similar encounter with God as I had just experienced. "I compare our thoughts to the traffic patterns we have in our homes. When we move the furniture, it often creates a new traffic pattern. When God rearranges the furniture within our heart, he creates new traffic patterns for our thoughts, causing them to be more aligned with His."

"Yes, that's exactly what it feels like. It felt like God was rearranging furniture in my brain. I never knew He could do that." I felt better, and from that point on, Wednesday mornings could not come soon enough. No matter how bad I felt physically, I didn't miss a Wednesday prayer time.

After a couple of weeks went by, I was convicted in my heart to share my story with my pastor's wife. No one at church knew that I had been abused or raped. No one knew that in my past I experienced countless nights drinking myself to sleep or snorting cocaine to escape emotional pain. One evening after the kids went to sleep, I pushed through the fatigue and pain and typed my story in detail. I finished around one in the morning and then climbed into bed. As I lay there, I thought about what I was about to share. *Am I crazy? What if the kids learn about my past? Even Tom doesn't know everything about me. What if people gossip about me, reject us? What if Tom is asked to step down as a deacon of the church? What if people won't let their children play with our children?*

I panicked and was overwhelmed with fear. Then, I felt a dark presence in the bedroom. It felt like it was hovering over me, trying to intimidate me. It worked. I could hardly breathe. I was paralyzed in fear and tried with all my might to move my arm to get Tom's attention, but my arm felt like it weighed a ton. I was terrified, and instinctively a faint whisper came out of my mouth, "Jesus," and the presence fled. He disappeared instantly. I woke Tom and told him what happened.

Tom pulled me in close to him, wrapped his arms around me, and prayed for me, reassuring me, "You're safe. He can't hurt you. He's just trying to intimidate you. I have a feeling your story is going to reach a lot of women who have been abused. Why else would Satan bother to intimidate you."

I fell asleep in Tom's arms, and the presence did not reappear that night. The next night, it returned very similarly to the night before.

Tom was out of town, and I prayed anxiously and intensely to myself, "Jesus, what do I do?"

Beyond the fear, I heard his instruction, "Worship Me."

I began to sing to Him worship songs, and the dark presence disappeared. Like a momma hen suspicious of prowling wolves, I went to each bedroom and retrieved my children, and brought them in bed with me. From that day on, worship music played in our house 24 hours a day. It became evident to me as well that something or someone did not want me to share my story.

The next morning, I emailed my story to our pastor's wife. *Here goes! It's either the best thing or the worst thing. But I can't sit on my story. I have to share it.*

I was relieved to get her call later that day because I was not sure how she would respond to knowing my past.

"Mary Ann, I had no idea that you suffered so much trauma in your life," were the first words I heard coming through my phone.

I was surprised by her response. *I suffered trauma? No. Trauma is for soldiers who see horrific horrors during a battle or war, or it's for those who suffer from a serious auto accident.*

"I don't know if you'd call it trauma, Diane. It was troubling," I responded.

Diane responded, "Girl, you suffered trauma, and it explains what you are experiencing now." *Really. So, what I am experiencing is real? Like, maybe it's ok, and I'm not a crazy basket case, after all.*

Diane was a nurse, and she and I talked about some simple and practical things that I could do to help relieve some of my symptoms and stress, like, take very short walks, look up into the blue sky, drink more water, breathe deeply. I hadn't realized until she mentioned it, but when I took a deep breath, I could feel that the impact of trauma reached deep to the core of my being. That was precisely what I was avoiding—The place that harbored my anger, resentment, bitterness, unforgiveness—and the most painful emotion—self-hatred. When I breathed deeply, I could almost touch the feelings I had stuffed for years. Outside I was 'fine' - inside, I was madder than 1,000 hornets. If you had asked me if I forgave anyone that hurt me, my response would have been, "Yes, of course." In my mind, I had forgiven, but my heart was revealing a different story.

I began reading Total Forgiveness. The author explained that the more someone suffers, the greater the blessing is waiting for them—*if* that person *totally* forgives. I read that forgiveness creates a changed life with great blessing, and…the magic word for me…*freedom.* I wasn't sure what freedom actually was and was curious if freedom was something I could experience consistently in my life. I had experiences with Jesus and the Holy Spirit, which caused me to feel free, but I had not truly walked in freedom. I felt I had a lot of work ahead of me because I had many people to forgive, including myself.

CRUSHED IN SPIRIT

Despite reading my bible daily, praying on Wednesdays, my debilitating fatigue and extreme exhaustion persisted. A verse in the Book of James seemed to jump off the page. *The sick are to be prayed for by the elders of the church.* Tom and I agreed that we would ask the pastors and elders to pray for me. Tom spoke to the lead pastor who assembled the pastors, Tom, the other elders, and their wives. They surrounded me in prayer. I sat exhausted in a chair in the midst of them.

As they prayed, I heard the wife of one of the deacons whisper to another, "I feel like Mary Ann is deeply tormented."

"Yes, I feel it too," I heard the other respond.

Tormented? Is that what I am feeling? How can that be? Who or what is tormenting me? Is it possible that I could be tormenting myself?

There were about ten people in the room, and each person prayed for me. I didn't know what to expect, but I was expectant. The last prayer prayed was by the pastor, "Therefore God exalted Jesus to the highest place and gave him the name that is above every name, and at the name of Jesus every knee should bow, in heaven and on earth and under the earth, and every tongue acknowledge that Jesus Christ is Lord, to the glory of God the Father. We are here to pray for healing for Mary Ann in the name of Jesus."

Immediately, whatever disorder or illness was lurking inside me literally fled my body like 1,000 hornets fleeing their nest. The heaviness was gone. The weight was gone. The darkness was gone. The fatigue was gone.

110

I looked up at everyone and shared in astonishment, "It fled! It's gone!"

They all hugged and celebrated with me and promised to continue to pray. I stood up and felt no fatigue, no pain, no heaviness. *It's gone. But what was it? What fled?*

Tom and Pastor David discussed that the battle wasn't over. The enemy wasn't giving up that easy. *The enemy? What enemy? Who is the enemy? And how does he get inside? How does he cause so much turmoil?*

Our pastor disrupted my thoughts, "Mary Ann, has God recently placed a scripture on your heart?"

"No, not really," I answered thoughtfully.

Tom interrupted, "Mary Ann, our kitchen is wallpapered with words from God."

We all laughed, and our pastor shared, "Good! That is your weapon right now. His Name and his Word. When you feel the enemy attacking you, hold that attack back with God's word. Speak God's word out loud. Listen to the words as you speak them. Declare them. Proclaim them. You are in a battle, and the truth is your weapon." *The truth is my weapon. Does that mean that the disorder was a lie? Maybe based on lies?*

I rehearsed our pastor's instructions in my mind, *Declare His Name, Proclaim His Word.* And added my own instruction *and Worship. Yes! Worship Jesus.*

I heard everyone talking with joy and saying their goodbyes as we left the church. The kids were asleep as we arrived home. Tom paid the babysitter, and I went upstairs to get ready for bed. I grabbed my Bible and fell into bed, holding it to my chest, and fell asleep. It would not be the last night I slept with my Bible held closely to my chest. I woke up early the next morning and made

111

my children their favorite breakfast, French Toast. Mommy's home!

MY KITCHEN WALLS EQUIPPED ME

Tom and our Pastor were right; the hornets came back, and so did the dark presence. Even though I felt small, vulnerable, and ill-equipped, my kitchen walls equipped me to win that battle. I could feel the illness try to invade my body through a slight pain or subtle weakness taking hold; I would walk into my kitchen and speak the verses God gave to me out loud until the weakness or pain left.

"Not by might, nor by power, but by my spirit." Zechariah 4:6

"Be strong and courageous! Do not be terrified nor dismayed, for the Lord your God is with you wherever you go." Joshua 1:9

"I am the good shepherd, and I know My own, and My own know Me." 1 John 10:14

"Call to Me and I will answer you, and I will tell you great and mighty things, which you do not know." Jeremiah 33:3

"Believe in the Lord Jesus Christ and you will be saved, you and your household." Acts 16:31

"The LORD is my light and my salvation; Whom shall I fear? The LORD is the defense of my life; Whom shall I dread?" Psalm 27:1

Faith in God's word and His truth was growing inside me. Standing firm on the words taped to my kitchen wall helped me concentrate on God's ability and His love for me rather than the fear of being sick again. Worship played throughout our house continually. Reading the Bible was a daily practice in our home, along with dancing and singing to Jesus. I guess they gave up, or maybe there was no place for them to invade because I no longer faced the 1,000 hornets of anger, the dark presence, the pain, the weakness, or the fatigue associated with whatever was plaguing me. That doesn't mean that I never was tired or ill, but I was never overcome by that sickness or disorder again.

My healing became known to our friends throughout the church, and I was asked to share my testimony publicly during a church service. As I shared the details of my life, the abuse, the beautiful message Tommy delivered to me that Jesus was God, the dream where Jesus told me to "be humble," the night he kneeled on the floor of my imprisoned heart and washed me clean. You could hear a pin drop. I couldn't discern if the people were bored and polite or if my story impacted them in some way.

After I completed my story, the response was surprising to me. I received hug after hug and many thanking me for being transparent and genuine about my past. Many confided that they too had been abused, were facing their own battles, and conveyed how much hope they felt by my story, and they too were encouraged to pursue a deeper relationship with Jesus.

Our Pastor thanked me for being humble and sharing things that were not easy. *I am beginning to understand that humility requires me to be transparent, honest, genuine, and truthful. And as difficult as that can be, it creates trust.*

Trust was becoming a beautiful by-product of humility.

HIS TENDER MERCY

God was rescuing me one step at a time. The anger I felt had caused great havoc to me personally and to my family, and while I was learning to deal with the warfare that surrounded it, my journey to evict it wasn't over. I knew that God was healing me, yet, I wasn't completely healed. I couldn't put my finger on it, but I sensed more emotional healing needed to come.

Prayer became my go-to. Helen and I had remained constant prayer warriors through our battles. Even though we were miles away, Helen has been a steadfast friend as we prayed together weekly by phone. Her love for the Word of God is contagious, and I never tire of hearing her proclaim it.

Lori, another life-long friend brought so much clarity and precision to our prayer time. When we prayed, a beautiful anointing was present that felt like soft morning rain.

Chris, a beautiful mother I met through our children's swim team, brought her gentle and kind spirit to the prayer time.

Barb has a voice like an angel who prays tenaciously until she sees or senses His answer. Susie shares tremendous value, wisdom, and insights from God's heart. God kept blessing me with women who pray.

I was 47, and Tom was 52 when we learned that we were pregnant. We had lost a baby two and one-half years earlier before we even knew we were pregnant with him. When he arrived in the world, he was approximately eight weeks. After he miscarried, I held his little body in the palm of my hand. His head was formed, and his skin was so transparent that I saw his little heart. We named him Matthew.

Now pregnant with our fifth child, we were thrilled to have one more opportunity to be parents. The doctor cautioned about low progesterone levels, and I began to visit his office weekly for progesterone shots. One afternoon during a sonogram appointment, the doctor searched and searched and searched and searched to find a heartbeat.

I looked at him knowingly and said, "We lost her, didn't we?"

Tears were in his eyes, "Yes, we did."

I was shocked at how emotionally moved he was. He hugged me and gently shared what the next few days would be like as Joy would have to be delivered even though no longer alive. I was shocked at how painful the delivery was; we weren't quite three months pregnant. After she was gone, we wept and wept and wept.

Tommy, Johnny, and Iris were terribly disappointed. Iris had been praying for a little sister. At 47 years old, knowing this would be the last opportunity I would be pregnant, I retreated to our bedroom and grieved. Tom was grieving as well; he would have ten children if God allowed it.

I begged God to return her, "You have the ability to put her back. I really want her, and I don't want to let her go. She's ours; why do we have to lose her!" I quarreled with God. I fasted and prayed. I just couldn't let go.

Then, with a swollen face from crying, I felt a breeze on my cheeks. *Lord, is that you?*

Peering through a lake of tears, I saw a vision right in front of me. It was a beautiful grassy knoll. The sky was an incredible blue; the grass was thick and lush. I could smell the freshness of the air as I saw a flowing gown from the waist down; someone was standing on a grassy knoll. It was Jesus. He wore a golden belt, and his gown was flowing in the breeze. I never saw His face, just his gown. I sat up as I saw a little girl holding on to his gown with her tiny fingers. She peered from behind his gown and looked me in the eyes. She was our baby. As she shyly looked at me, I knew she was His more than she was mine. She was so beautiful. Her soft blonde hair and big round brown eyes spoke to me. She loved Him, and she didn't want to leave Him. I had never considered that she was in Heaven and would have wanted to stay. She was safe. She was loved. I sat in my bed and thought, "I will see her again." Tom named her Joy. Jesus had graciously comforted me and encouraged me with the truth. Joy was Home.

MAKE THIS A HOUSE OF PRAYER

"Make this a House of Prayer." I felt these words whisper upon my heart while reading my Bible.

They were imprinted on my heart and mind, and I shared them with Tom and our friend Mark, who was also a pastor.

Mark's face lit up with a big smile, and he responded by saying, "Are the Otleys ready for a road trip?"

Tom said, "Sure! Where to?"

Mark smiled his big smile and answered, "We are going to take you to the International House of Prayer (IHOP-KC)."

The following Friday, each family had their vans packed with kids and suitcases and on our way to Kansas City to experience which would become one of my greatest treasures while living in Missouri, the International House of Prayer in Kansas City.

The IHOP prayer room is a unique place. Since 1999, IHOP-KC has faithfully prayed and worshipped 24 hours a day, 7 days a week. It is a sacred place, and when I stepped into the prayer room for the first time, I felt peace. While sitting in the prayer room in the midst of worship and prayer, hours seemed like minutes, and the presence of God was evident. Only three and a half hours away from our home, it became the perfect weekend getaway. It became a place of retreat and reprieve. When it was clear that I needed time to get away, I spent my "me-time" in the prayer room, with bible, journal, and pen in hand; I drew near to God, praying, waiting, and listening for His guidance.

Our family was greatly influenced by the worship songs written and performed by gifted intercessory missionaries like Misty Edwards, Cory Asbury, Sarah Edwards, Matt Gilman, Jonas Park, Justin Rizzo, Jay Thomas, Jon Thurlow, Jason Upton, Luke Wood, and The Merchant Band. Our kids actually picked up playing guitar just by watching these missionaries play. It was an electric time to be a believer in Jesus Christ. This worship filled our hearts and home with adoration for God, the Holy Spirit, and Jesus.

Visiting IHOP and having the prayer room streamed into our home drew us into deeper intimacy with God. For me, Jon Thurlow's sets were especially beneficial. As I dialed down and soaked in the soft melodies and beautiful love songs to God, I would experience peace, comfort, connection, intimacy, and healing that only God Himself could provide.

It was also a time that helped me greatly appreciate prayer. I was greatly encouraged by reading Jim Cymbala's *Fresh Wind, Fresh Fire*, a first-hand account of how the Brooklyn Tabernacle Church and the Brooklyn Tabernacle Choir were built on the foundation of prayer. The miracles represented in that book inspired me to trust God in a new way. I began to read classic books on prayer by Andrew Murray, E.M. Bounds, and J.C. Ryle. Stormie Omartian's, The Power of a Praying Wife lay at my bedside table. Prayer became my heartbeat. Tom and I became committed to prayer and became leaders in the National Day of Prayer and the Governor's Prayer Team. As you will see, it would be prayer that would eventually lead me on a path to deep healing and restoration.

DAD DID LOVE ME

During one weekend at the House of Prayer, something very unexpected happened. While enjoying the solitude, I sat with my pen and journal, waiting to hear from the Holy Spirit. But God didn't speak to me; He did the unexpected – He showed me a vision. I saw my Dad in a department store looking for a turntable. He really wanted to be certain that he bought the "right" one. *Oh, my goodness, he is picking out my sixteenth birthday present!*

Then I saw him flipping through albums, looking for just the right one. He was troubled because he didn't know what music I liked. I could sense he didn't want me to be disappointed. I instantly was convicted of how I arrogantly made fun of the Carpenters Album Dad had given me. The reality shocked me; *Oh my God, Dad loved me. I had no idea!*

Then God shared with me something, tenderly, but directly. "You were rebellious."

And I retorted abruptly, "Of course I was, I mean, who wouldn't be! Did you see what he did to me?"

God responded, "Your dad is responsible for his sin, and you are responsible for yours. Ask him to forgive you for being rebellious."

In an instant, memories flooded back of times I blatantly disobeyed Dad, outwardly displaying hatred toward him and lying to him, sneering at him, and despising him. I tucked God's instruction in my heart and told God, "I'm nervous, and I don't know how, but I'll do it," knowing that God would provide the time and the courage, I returned home to my family.

I shared the vision with Tom, and we agreed that I would go to see Dad when we both felt it was the right time.

THE ANCIENT PATH

I was fifty years old, and out of nowhere, I had a recurring dream. In it, I was standing at an intersection of two major highways. They were made of concrete and were built high above the ground. They were impressive and boasted of breathtaking travels. My dilemma was, which highway do I take? Do I go North, South, East, or West? I ran down each highway, trying to understand the best way. *Where am I supposed to go?* The pressure was unsettling. *What if I make a mistake? What if I go the wrong way? What will I miss?*

Behind me, in the distance below, on the side of the huge intersection, near a forest, I saw Jesus standing in front of a narrow path that led into the woods. Jesus kept beckoning to me to come to Him. He wanted me to follow Him and travel with Him on that narrow path that led into the woods.

Standing near the intersection, I would explain to Jesus, "No! I can't go that way. I have to be on the *main* highway. I have to be in the mainstream. Your path leads to nowhere. I need to go somewhere big!"

This dream re-occurred so many times that it became troubling.

Tom and I were the Coordinators for Missouri National Day of Prayer and organized a 24-hour prayer event at the Arch in St. Louis. Madge, one of the worship leaders at the event, brought an elderly lady who was suffering from rheumatoid arthritis. She was frail; her back was bent over; her fingers were inflamed and misshaped.

"Mary Ann, this Elsie. She is a very good friend of mine, and she wanted to be here with us to pray for the City."

"Hello, Elsie, it's so nice to meet you. I am glad you came to join us."

Elsie looked up at me, and as our eyes met, she spoke to me directly and intently, "Mary Ann, I can help you with your deliverance."

I was immediately offended.

My deliverance. What is she talking about? Is there something obvious about me that insinuates I need deliverance? Who is this lady?

119

She smiled at me, and I politely thanked her for joining us before returning to my responsibilities at the event.

That was odd.

Worship filled the air, and prayers were expressed for the city and the outlying areas to know Jesus as their healer, their help, their deliverer, and the lover of their souls. Once the Arch Event ended, we noticed that Madge had left a cooler behind. We called Madge and agreed to drop it off at a church where she was attending a seminar. The church was located on our way home. We arrived at Life Church during the conclusion of the seminar.

Tom took the cooler into the church and was given a Pastor's packet describing the seminar, which included a book. When we got back in our car to return home, Tom handed the book to me. As it sat in my lap, I looked at the cover of the book and was speechless.

"Are you OK?" Tom asked.

"I'm not sure. Look at this cover?" I answered.

Tom looked at me and read the title, "Ancient Path," and waited for an explanation.

"You know that dream that has been troubling me? The one about the highways and the path?" I explained.

"I think so," he answered.

"Look at this picture. This path is the same path that Jesus is calling to me to go on in my dream."

"I'd say you better read the book," Tom answered. I agreed.

The next day was Mother's Day, and after we ate the delicious breakfast Tom and the kids made for me, I headed for the backyard to settle into my favorite Mother's Day present ever, a beautiful hammock. *I'm going to find out what this book is about.*

Once I opened it, I couldn't put it down. The whole time my children were trying to celebrate me, I wept and wept.

"Mary Ann, what about this book is causing you to feel this way?" Tom asked, concerned.

"Tom, I am reading my story in this book. I understand what happened to me. And I know that there are deep wounds inside me that need to be healed," I answered.

The book explains that in the Old Testament of the Bible, a prophet named Jeremiah spoke these words to God's people, "Thus says the Lord, 'Stand by the ways, and see, and ask for the ancient paths, where the good way is, and walk in it; and you shall find rest for your souls.' But they *(the Israelites)* said, 'We will not walk in it.'"

When I first read the verse, I thought, "How defiant are those people! Why wouldn't they listen to God?"

Then, I was reminded of my dream, where God was standing by the way, inviting me to travel an ancient path with Him, and I answered the same as the Israelites, "I will not walk in it."

Uh-oh.

As I continued to read, I discovered the ancient path that God revealed to the Israelites was a concealed, hidden, and eternal path. It's not a path we can create or manufacture. It's a path that we need to seek, and he needs to reveal. This Ancient Path would ensure our lives be pleasant, agreeable, prosperous, and distinguished.

121

Ironically, these were all the things I was looking for on the main highways

I was amazed! God designed this path to be imparted and passed from generation to generation. Without it, our personal, cultural, spiritual, emotional, financial, family and health needs go unmet. Instead of being God-focused and other-focused, we become self-focused and lose sight of the path that brings us what we need. The ancient path is imparted by the parents, primarily by the father, in the form of blessings.

The blessings are basically positive and encouraging words, sentiments, beliefs, actions toward the children. The path is based on parents agreeing with God about their children's value and identity and imparting those truths to their children. There are specific times when specific blessings are to be imparted, like conception, birth, adolescence, early adulthood, marriage, etc. At these times, the parents were to impart a blessing in thought, word, and deed that would communicate to their children and the world around them that the child was affirmed in their identity—being accepted, loved, cherished, wanted, prized, and valuable.

I learned that blessing our children was actually a lifestyle—a lifestyle that agreed with God's heart about each child's value, which, when communicated, impacted the trajectory of their lives. This ancient secret was true then and is true today. The blessings we impart to our children establish their identity and purpose. Knowing their identity and purpose is a firm foundation upon which to grow into the adults God intended them to be. Conversely, when we curse our children, the opposite of blessing will occur; they will believe the lie that they are not accepted, that they are unlovable and not valuable. I was stunned!

Me. Deep down, I am not convinced that I am loved, accepted or valuable.

Craig Hill, the author, then gave a common example of how we can leave the ancient path. His example was a story of a teenage girl who was wounded by her father. Because she is wounded, she enters into rebellion against him and cuts off her relationship with him. She steps outside the circle of blessing and protection God designed for her. Having been deeply wounded by her father, the girl now goes out in search of love. She meets a boy who says he loves her. Because of the hurt she feels, she allows herself to be sexually involved. He explains the short-sighted pattern of her choices; a spiraling sequence of disappointments occurring with each choice she made with hope for deliverance from her previous decision led to even greater disappointment and ultimately despair. The quest for love ends in guilt and shame. The girl lives in continual search and survival mode; she has no peace, no feeling of value. She feels no love. In the Book of Jeremiah, God states that men's hearts were hardened, and they forgot how to blush. Nothing was sacred anymore.

Dad and me? Had Dad's heart hardened? Had he forgotten how to blush? Did he seek a different path, and end up wounding me in the process?

While reading this book, I discovered that I was influenced by the belief that the "good life" is about getting what I think I want. But look around; the people that get all that they wish for are not necessarily the happiest. Look at Hollywood as one example. No matter where you're born or what your expectation is, outside of God and the ancient paths He has established, there is no "good life."

One of the most helpful statements that I read about the "reality of life" is that we are born into the middle of a battle. A battle between two kingdoms. God's Kingdom—the Kingdom of Light, and God's enemy's kingdom—the kingdom of darkness. These two kingdoms are continually at war, and the territory they are warring over is our minds and hearts. Both play very differently. Both play for keeps. Both play to the end. One kingdom is based on truth, the other deception. One is based on love, the other fear. One blesses, the other curses.

I thought back to my childhood. I recognized the pull on Dad's heart even then. He loved us; I have no question about that. But somehow, it was apparent to even me that he was in a battle, and the enemy was winning.

If the kingdom of darkness influenced Dad to the point that he lost his sense of boundaries and judgment, could he still be influenced by the Kingdom of Light and set free from his bondage? I don't know how You will accomplish this, but with all my heart, I'm hoping you can still reach him, God.

Instead of eating lunch at a nice restaurant and spending the day planting flowers in the front yard (my traditional Mother's Day activities), I read and wept and read and wept until I completed the book. After much grieving, I accepted that I had to release the father-daughter relationship that I had secretly wanted to have with Dad even after all these years. I would find the blessing that I missed from Dad from my heavenly Father, and I would learn to bless my family as well. As for Dad, I released him from his responsibility to parent me as a daughter. From now on, I would be his intercessor. I would pray that God's will would be done in my Dad's life.

A little disturbed by my reaction to the book and the disappointing Mother's Day, Tom took the book with him as he left for New York the following morning. He read the book in one sitting and called me when his plane landed.

"I understand why you were so upset. *Ancient Paths* is a powerful book. It's timely and brings up very good points we need to consider going forward. I want to learn how to bless our family the way God intends and impart God's identity and destiny to our children," he explained.

"Me too, Sweetheart, me too," I answered.

Tom went on to explain, "This book has a companion seminar. When I return from New York, I am going to research the seminar and decide if we should attend."

"Sounds good," I answered.

Within weeks of Tom's return, we attended the Ancient Path Seminar by Family Foundations International. It was hosted by Life Church just minutes from our home. In the seminar, Craig Hill, the author of the book and seminar, explained in greater detail about God's ancient paths of blessing and how important it is to know God's true loving nature. He shared how important it is to our children's identity that we agree with God's thoughts and heart toward ourselves, our children, and each other. I recognized how I had been influenced early in my life by the false teaching that God was disappointed with me and that He would punish me. Even though I had amazing encounters with Jesus, there existed a little part of my heart that still believed God secretly hated me. I was about to find out why.

After session one, we broke into groups for prayer. Tom and I entered the prayer room that we were assigned, and you will never guess who was there. Sitting in one of the chairs was Elsie, the little old lady who had visited the Arch to pray with us. The lady I was so offended by because she told me that she could help me with my deliverance. I didn't know then, but God had sent one of his strongest warriors to lovingly guide me into His freedom.

Seven of us sat in a circle while Elsie led us in prayer. She asked each of us what our first memory of God or hearing about God was. We all shared our experiences. And then she led us in prayer by merely asking, "Father, please share with us what you want us to know."

I kept my eyes closed and heard someone's voice. It was low, quiet, and broken, intermixed with tears. It was Tom's. Elsie asked if he would like to share what the Holy Spirit was revealing to him.

Tom responded by saying, "No. I need to talk to my wife."

Tom turned to me, took my hands in his, and said, "Mary Ann, I have not honored you as I should—I have been selfish and have not considered your needs. Please forgive me."

Immediately, I broke into uncontrollable tears. Tom was so good to me in so many ways; I never wanted to bring up that he could also be terse and demanding, insensitive to my needs.

Elsie led Tom in prayer, and Tom asked God and me to forgive him and told me that he was going to rely on God's love and guidance in our marriage from now on. Only God knows the needs of each human heart, marriage, and relationship. Only God could have known the secret longings of my heart for my marriage and touch Tom so tenderly, without condemnation, but with revelation.

It gets better.

The next night of the seminar, after the teaching, we broke into groups again. After experiencing the power of the prayer time, I anticipated what others might experience during this time. As Elsie opened the prayer time, I felt a memory well up inside of me.
Oh, no.

I fought it and kept pushing it down, but I couldn't.

Tears were streaming down my face.

"It looks like the Holy Spirit may be revealing something to you, Mary Ann. Would you like to pray about it?" Elsie asked.

"I don't know," I answered uncomfortably.

Elsie positioned a stool in front of me, sat down, and asked permission to hold my hands. I agreed, and she held my hands in her soft curled hands and asked, "Holy Spirit, would you please reveal to Mary Ann why she is crying." Immediately, I saw in my mind a memory of being 13 years old, that first horrible night when Dad entered my room.

"I can't go here. I have been to psychologists and counselors. They all want me to go back to this place, but I can't. It only makes matters worse."

Elsie looked at me empathetically, "I understand," she answered. She looked at me resolutely and asked, "What if we let Jesus do the work this time? Would you be willing to let Him?"

"Can he do that?" I asked curiously.

"Yes, He can," she responded confidently.

I wasn't exactly sure what that meant, I whispered, "OK, I'll try."

Elsie gently held my hands and asked me, "What is the Holy Spirit showing you?"

I closed my eyes, and I was back in the vision of being in my bedroom the first night dad had come into my room. I stayed silent.

"Mary Ann, what are you feeling?" Elsie asked.

My heart was racing; I felt like recoiling.

"I'm scared," the words came out unexpectedly.

Elsie continued to hold my hands, "what else are you feeling?"

"I am ashamed. I am afraid I am in trouble. I am afraid my Mom is going to be really mad. I am afraid if someone finds out what will happen to Dad ... and what will happen to me? I am afraid that I caused this. I am terrified!"

Elsie was not moved and gently asked, "Dear, what is causing you to feel these emotions?"

Feeling like a 13-year-old, I didn't know how to explain the memory. I was so ashamed, and I struggled to articulate what I experienced.

"Let's pray," Elsie suggested, and she told God exactly what I told her.

"Father, this dear one, your daughter... *I don't feel like anyone's daughter...* She is scared. She feels ashamed of what happened. She fears that she is in trouble, that her mom is going to be upset with her. She doesn't know that will happen to her Dad and her."

I felt heard for the first time; understood, validated. Elsie didn't add or detract from what I shared. She simply told God what I told her. Elsie didn't diagnose me or prescribe a solution. She simply shared with God the emotions that I had shared with her, the deep feelings I had stuffed down and bottled up for almost 40 years.

She ended the prayer by asking Jesus, "Lord Jesus, what do you want Mary Ann to know?" and she waited. And I waited to hear God respond to this incredible prayer.

"Dear, what is Jesus showing you," Elsie asked gently. I explained that I had arrived home from babysitting one night, had gone to bed, and woke up to my Dad in my bed, touching me in private places. Sharing with this level of trust was a space I had never been in before. I trusted her.

I was crying heavily when Elsie explained, "Mary Ann, I am going to ask Jesus to reveal to you what is happening."

I looked at her, puzzled.

Isn't it a little obvious what is happening?

As if to read my mind, Elsie instructed, "Listen for Jesus."

I had already opened this can of worms. There is no turning back now.

"OK, I will," I whispered.

Elsie repeated to Jesus what I was feeling, "Jesus, Mary Ann feels trapped and confused. She is afraid for herself, her family, and her dad. She feels responsible, and she's really, really afraid. She is afraid of what her mother will think, and she is terrified."

As I listened to Elsie talk to God again, I felt validated. And I was surprised that she was talking to Jesus as if he was sitting right next to us. As Elsie was relaying my feelings to Jesus, she didn't judge me. I felt like she was the first person that genuinely heard me and understood what I felt. She went on to ask, "Jesus, will you please tell Mary Ann what is going on in that room?"

My eyes were closed, and I intently listened for Jesus. But He didn't speak to me. Instead, He showed me vision, a vision of that night. It was as if I was living it over again. But there was something very different this time. This time, Jesus was in the room.

"Elsie, Jesus is in the room."

"That's good," she said patiently, "Pay attention to Him."

With my eyes closed, I watched Jesus. He was clothed in a beautiful white garment. For a moment, I felt comforted and safe.

I heard Elsie ask, "Jesus, what do you want Mary Ann to know about this night?"

My eyes were clenched tight, just like they were that night, and now I was filled with anxiety; I waited for what would happen next.

"Elsie! There is someone else in the room!" I exclaimed horrifically.

Behind dad, a giant, wasp-like, roach-like demon towered.

"Elsie, a demon is towering over Dad and me. He's like 9 feet tall. He looks like a giant creepy wasp or roach. He's intimidating!"

He was disgusting, vile, and looming over Dad. I recognized how I felt around this spirit.

"Elsie, this demon has intimidated me all of my life." I recognized its polluted toxins filling the air.

And all this time, I had thought it was Dad.

"He is so evil, so wicked."

As I was describing to Elsie what I was witnessing, I thought, *What in the world is going to happen now?! He could eat Jesus for lunch.*

Elsie calmly asked, "Jesus, what do you want to do with this wasp-like, roach-like demon that is towering over Mary Ann's dad and intimidating Mary Ann?"

Quite frankly, when I heard Elsie ask Jesus what He wanted to do with this demon, I was afraid for Jesus' safety. I thought it was over for Jesus. Then I saw Jesus approach the demon. He held a push pin in his fingers, and he simply poked the demon in the stomach and pinned him to the wall. Jesus had literally pinned the demon to the wall. The demon was angry and madly tried to fight his way out from under that pin, but he could not escape.

Then Jesus looked at me and said emphatically, "He will never torment you again."

"Elsie, Jesus just pinned that demon to the wall. That thing looked so big, and now he is so minuscule. How did he make himself look so large?" I asked.

"The enemy is full of deception and lies. He is no match for Jesus. If Jesus pinned him to the wall, I guarantee you, that is where he will stay."

I could breathe easier now.

Elsie reached out and held my hands again; I closed my eyes and found myself back in the room as she prayed, "Jesus, what do you want Mary Ann to know about her father?"

I saw Dad. He didn't look so intimidating anymore. He looked broken. I was waiting to hear Jesus tell me what he wanted me to know about Dad, and I thought he might say something like, "His punishment is up to me. Vengeance is Mine. I will repay." But something very different happened. There was intentional silence, a pause, and I took my eyes off Dad and looked to Jesus.

I saw love in Jesus' eyes. I could see what Jesus saw. He was looking past all things people see, the horrible stuff, and looked right into my dad's heart. I looked at Dad and now saw a little boy, and I noticed that that little boy was just as confused about life as I was. I saw years of strife and struggle, years of pride and anger, years of counterfeit answers. Then Jesus shared something with me that forever changed my heart.

I heard Elsie ask, "Jesus, who is Mary Ann's dad to you?"

Jesus turned to look at me and answered unashamedly, "He is my son."

I cannot put on paper the love that I witnessed in His eyes. I can just say that it changed my heart forever. I was comforted by it. His love is powerful, and because of his great love, he pinned the mastermind of Dad's perversion to the wall. I fell in love with Jesus' heart and told Elsie, "He is not ashamed of Dad. Dad is forgiven. He loves Dad, Elsie."

There is hope for Dad.

I shared with Elsie all that I had just experienced, and she replied, "Mary Ann, can you forgive your Dad?"

And I responded, "Yes, 100%, 150%. I forgive Dad."

I had a new perspective on the Kingdom of Darkness. Its influence is real. If Dad had known that that power over him could have easily been overcome by Jesus, his life and our family would be in a different place.

"I had no idea he was enslaved to this darkness, Elsie."

My heart grieved that Dad had not followed God's Ancient Paths but had hope that there was still hope.

Elsie encouraged me to ask Jesus a question, "Mary Ann, ask Jesus who you are to Him."

I recalled the very night we were now visiting; after Dad had left the room, I clung to my pillow in fear and heard a voice speak to me, "You must really be bad for something like this to happen." I felt dejected and did not want to ask Jesus who I was to Him.

"Elsie, I know what God thinks of me. We don't have to go there. We don't have to ask him," secretly, I couldn't bear to hear it again.

Elsie replied, "Mary Ann, it's really important that you ask Him this question."

I trusted her and stirred up the courage to ask Jesus who I was to Him. I was reluctant.

I expected Jesus to say, "Listen, girl, if you would just cooperate with me, if you would just obey Me from now on, if you would get your act together, I can squeak you in. But girl, you have got to…"

So, with clenched eyes, waiting for the hammer to drop. I went back to the bedroom memory and asked Jesus, "Who do You say I am?"

In response to my question, I was now alone with Jesus. Dad was gone. The demon was gone. Jesus and I were in the bedroom where my identity as a "bad" girl was established. Jesus and I were facing each other. *Jesus is so beautiful.* He wasn't mad or frustrated with me. Instead, He approached me with a garment in his hands. It was a simple but beautiful white robe.

Like a father would place a dress over his child, Jesus placed the robe over my head. I felt beautiful, prized, treasured, whole, and cleansed. Then he placed a gold crown on my head. The gold was pure and transparent; you could see through it. It sat perfectly on my head, and I stood up straight and felt a sense of dignity.

Jesus took a beautiful ring and lovingly placed it on my finger, and I felt betrothed. I belonged to Him. He knelt and placed sandals on my feet. They were a perfect fit, and I felt like I was standing on firm ground. They gave me purpose.

Then Jesus took my hands in His, looked lovingly into my eyes, and repeated my question, "Who are you to Me?"

There was a beautiful pause as I felt the majesty of the moment, then he lovingly answered, "You are My princess."

133

I was overwhelmed by His love. I was astounded by His acceptance. I fell into His arms. He held me, and I never felt so valued in all my life. I didn't know this kind of love existed. He blessed me and established my identity as His princess. He washed away the lies the demon had whispered in my heart almost 40 years earlier – I am not a bad girl. I am accepted, I am prized, I am cherished, I am a princess. I wept uncontrollably while Tom, Elsie, and the others prayed around me, patiently allowing me to have my time with my beautiful savior.

The darkness and perversion that once permeated the room from my childhood were gone. Brilliant light, unconditional love, safety, respect, dignity, and honor filled the room. Heaven filled the room and cleansed my 13-year-old wounded heart. Now when I look back to the most traumatic memory of my life, I see Jesus. I see me. I see light. I see love.

It isn't about being bad or good. It's about being loved. That's how He makes all things new.

A RECORD OF MY SINS

Before the end of the Ancient Path seminar, I had shared my story with the entire group of participants. I shared details of my story that I had not told before. I was completely transparent and then shared how during this seminar, Jesus came to me, clothed me in honor, treated me with the highest dignity, and established my identity.

When I sat down, I was surprised by how I felt. I thought I would feel relieved, but I panicked. My face was flushed and hot. I wanted to run out of the room. Charles, a leader in the church, came to me and asked if I was OK.

I confided, "Charles, I think I made a big mistake. What if my children find out about my past? What if people reject us because of my past?"

Charles looked down at a binder he was carrying. He ripped a page from the binder, folded it, and handed it to me. "Mary Ann, this is a record of your sins," he said as he walked away.

You took notes? Who does that?

I sat back down and held the folded piece of paper in my hand. I had to know what he could possibly have written down after hearing my story. I opened it and stared at the page in confusion. The page was blank.

I stood up and rushed to Charles, "Charles, this page is blank. I don't understand," I asked.

Charles answered with a smile, "Mary Ann, there is no record of your sins. They have been removed as far as the east is from the west. What you do have is a testimony of God's love. Don't be intimidated by the past; embrace the beauty of your story, and the calling God has on your life."

Charles has since passed away, but I still have that piece of paper stuck in my Bible. To share this lesson I learned, I published a book called "A Book of Remembrance: The Record of My Sins." It is comprised of blank pages to remind us that every day every sin is forgiven, and we are washed clean by the blood of Jesus. I printed 100 copies and gave them away as gifts. Elsie shared that book all over the world as she ministered to people. She said she often shared it with people the same way Charles shared that piece of paper with me and loved to see the look on their faces when they figured out the same truth that Charles had taught me. Through Jesus, we are forgiven; there is no record.

HE MAKES ALL THINGS NEW

A painful and awkward part of my story is that I became more and more aware of another unresolved issue in my life — the secret hatred I felt toward my body. I was first introduced to

Playboy Bunnies when Dad watched Playboy on TV. At a young age, I recall comparing myself to their perfect bodies, perfect hair, perfect makeup, and perfect smiles. They were beautiful, and I ... was not. And after being abused, I felt like trash. I was embarrassed and uncomfortable with my body. I felt that my body should be separate from me, and that was a problem because it went with me wherever I went. No matter how I tried to look or feel different, I had the same body. It was time to face it. My hatred for my body was interfering with my marriage and getting in the way of our intimacy. I told Tom that I was struggling and feeling ugly, fat, motherly, and not attractive.

"Mary Ann, you are more attractive to me than the day I met you," he always replied. But it was very hard for me to accept.

Tom and I prayed and asked God to help. We both had learned to ask and listen. I heard Jesus say to me, "We are going on an adventure." With Tom holding my hand and with my eyes closed in prayer, Jesus appeared and took me on a tour of my body from the inside out. He showed me how marvelous my brain was designed, He showed me how fascinating my heart was as it pumped blood throughout my body, He took me through my reproductive organs and shared how miraculous my body was to carry children. Every part of my body was pure and beautiful to Jesus. He was not ashamed of me, and He was proud of the wondrous works of my human body. He gave me a completely different perspective of my body that night. His respect for me inside-out transformed the way I think of everyone's body. It's not how tall, short, thin, or voluptuous a person is; it's how absolutely miraculous our bodies are made.

Jesus brought women and resources into my life to help me understand that He has a design for everything, including sexual intimacy. And that in everything He designs, His love and His goodness are available. Step-by-step, as I took each of the images of being raped and being abused to Jesus, He created healing. When I look back to each of those instances, I now see light. I remember them still, but I am not alone in the story. I am not vulnerable - I am rescued. I am not fearful - I am abiding in His strength. Jesus is there. Love is there. Forgiveness is there.

God has helped me understand the beauty of sexual intimacy and the sacredness of being intimate with my husband. On my website, lovetriumphs.com, I share resources that have been valuable to me in gaining an understand God's perspective on sexual intimacy. We can enjoy freedom and beauty in God's design for our lives.

LOVE TRIUMPHS

I accompanied my children to their piano lessons each week and, Miss Diane, their piano teacher, sensed that I would like to learn as well.

"Mary Ann, I keep watching you watch those piano keys. Would you like me to teach you to play?"

"Do you think I am too old?" I asked.

"Absolutely not," she answered.

At 53 years old, I began the process. I fumbled and sounded clunky. I wanted to play beautiful melodies, but it took time.

Finally, I learned chords and would get up in the morning to play and worship Jesus. One morning, while worshiping, I asked Him to help me write a song to Him. Soon after, a melody came to me. I hummed it to my kids, and they helped me find the keys that matched the melody. Tommy wrote the music for me on paper. And one evening, I woke up in the middle of the night, quietly walked downstairs, sat at the kitchen table, and wrote the words to my song to Jesus:

137

Love Triumphs!

I sighed; You heard
I cried; You answered me.

He lied; I believed.
He tried to steal my destiny.

But love triumphed against my foe.
Love triumphed, and you call me Your own.

And now I know you heard my sighs
And now I know you saved me

And now I know you heard my cries
And now I know you love me, you love me!

Love triumphed against my foe
Love triumphed, and now … I know.

I had searched for answers, and now I know. The answers lie not in a lifestyle but in a person. The person who created me. The answers are not difficult or complicated, or impossible. They are simple. He is love, and His love triumphs.

Now I know the answer to questions that I screamed to the sky three decades prior. What's real? What's important? What's the truth?

What's real? God is real.

What's important? People are most important to God. I am important to Him. You are important to Him.

What's the truth? Jesus is the Son of God. He came to rescue humanity from a universe full of transgressions. There is nothing He cannot redeem.

I have shared my story in high schools, middle schools, colleges, jails, conferences, and churches. I will never forget a young student longing for truth. After hearing my story during a school assembly, she asked if she could talk with me. Jill and I met privately as she cried and shared her story.

"I was dating a guy that I thought I was in love with." Her eyes were so young, her heart so tender.

"I got pregnant. And I knew my dad would kill me, and if not me, definitely my boyfriend. So, I went to an abortion clinic. They told me that it was probably a false pregnancy, and they would do a test. After the test was complete, they told me that false pregnancies were common and that I wasn't pregnant yet, but they found a piece of tissue, and they recommend it be removed by a simple procedure, just in case. For $450, they would remove it, and my problems would be solved. My boyfriend got the money from somewhere and broke up with me. I took the money and went to have the procedure because I was afraid to tell my parents why I had gone there in the first place."

It hurt my heart to hear how alone she was in this experience.

"While I was there, it felt wrong, and yet I didn't know how to leave. As I lay on the table, they took an instrument, put it inside of me, and pulled something out. They placed it in a glass bowl. While they finished the procedure, the person next to me told me to look ahead, but I had to look. So, I glanced over the bowl and saw blood and what looked like a blob. As I stared, I realized it was a tiny human. I was shocked because I realized I just had an abortion. I became so sick to my stomach that I wanted to run and throw up. I tried to hold it together. When it was all done, I rushed out of the office. A friend was waiting for me outside and drove me home. I couldn't stop screaming, 'They killed my baby! I killed my baby! Why?! Why didn't they tell me it was a baby! Why would they do that?' I can't get the memory of that baby out of my mind!" She sobbed.

I held her hand, and then, as gently as I could, I asked, "Do you feel responsible?"

She cried harder, "Yes! I am responsible!"

"Would you be willing to tell Jesus that you feel responsible?" I asked.

She nodded through her tears. "Jesus, I am so sorry. I am so sorry. How could I be so stupid? What have I done?"

I gently guided her, "Jill, have you invited Jesus into your life to be your Savior."

"Yes," she nodded.

"So, you know that He came to this earth to rescue us when we are lost, even when we rebel from what He has called us to do?"

"Yes," she whispered.

"Let's ask Him if He is angry with you."

Jill cried, "Jesus, are You angry with me?"

I waited while holding her hand and then asked, "What did you hear?"

She answered in disbelief, "I felt like He said He has never been angry with me and that He loves me. Can that be possible?"

I answered her, "It is absolutely possible. How does it feel that He is not angry with you?"

"It feels good," she answered, wiping streams of tears from her face.

"Is there something else that you would like to ask Him?" I asked.

"Yes," Jill answered, breaking into a loud cry, "Where is my baby?"

I held her hand tightly, "Let's ask Him," I answered.

Jill sat up, took a deep breath as if to muster the courage, and through heavy sobs asked, "Jesus, where is my baby?"

We sat in silence as tears streamed down her eyes. She looked up at me, her voice filled with hope, "He has her. I saw her. She's beautiful. She is safe. Jesus has her," she responded incredulously. Jill looked as if she had 100 pounds of weight removed from her shoulders.

"Let's thank Him." Jill and I both thanked Jesus for sharing this beautiful truth with us.

"Jill, is there anything else you would like to ask Jesus," I asked?

"Yes," she replied, "Jesus, will you please forgive me?" We waited in silence while tears streamed down her face until she looked up and repeated the words, He spoke to her, and she received his response, "Forgiven."

We both smiled at each other. "Jill, let's ask Jesus one more question. Remember in my story when Elsie encouraged me to ask Jesus who I was to Him?"

"Yes," she answered.

"Ask Jesus who are you to Him."

"Jill sat up straight again. Wiped her tears, blew her nose, and asked, "Jesus, who am I to you?" It took courage, and I knew it. I had been in her shoes years before - filled with guilt and shame yet needing to hear the truth from God about who I *really* am. Again, tears streamed down from her eyes. In response to her prayer, she dug out a notebook from her backpack.

She wrote the date on the top of a page and wrote on the first line, "I am His Beautiful Daughter."

She looked at me and smiled, "I bought this journal because I heard that journaling was important but didn't know what to write in it. I think this is a good beginning."

Her eyes were bright. Her head was lifted. Jesus filled her heart with love. Jill had a deep longing for truth, and as she courageously searched for answers, she found the Truth. The Truth revealed the *truth* to her about her identity and her unborn child's. The Truth showed her the *way* to forgiveness so she could have a *life* filled with peace. Jesus is the Truth, the Way, and the Life. We finished with Jill telling Jesus that she wanted to be His for the rest of her life.

"Show me the way," she humbly asked.

The more I pray with others, the more I appreciate the truth Jesus was very clear about. He has an enemy, and that enemy is as at war with us. This enemy has no conscience and no mercy. He intentionally targets us when we are young and vulnerable. It is his goal to fill our young and impressionable minds with thoughts of fear, doubt, discouragement, self-hatred, and death. His goal is to convince us that we are not lovable. Who he is, how he influences others to treat us, and the dark cloud of despair he loves to hang over us is separate from who we are. His identity and ours are not the same. The enemy is totally dark. But because Jesus dwells within us, we are light. Our true identity is in Jesus...This is the most important truth for me to hang on to—In Christ, I am loved, and I am a light.

When my mind is filled with condemning thoughts, and I feel convinced that I am worthless and undeserving of love; when I am filled with despair, discouragement, and disappointment; when my emotions are filled with fear, anguish, or self-hatred, I have to dig deeper for Jesus. I need to draw near to Him and hold on to the underlying truth—that essential, foundational, basic, core truth that God is Love and that His love is bigger than the lies that are trying to drown out my value. God's love is bigger than the wrongs I have done and have been done to me. I cannot lift the heaviness myself, but He can. He can pin the enemy to the wall, and He can lift my head. Jesus is the Truth, and the Truth is that each of us is extravagantly loved, and there is nothing that He cannot do or will not do to redeem you and me.

What's real? God is.

What's important? We are.

What's the truth? We are never alone. We have Jesus.

The Triumph

Tom and I both sensed God's leading that now, after several years, was the time I should see my Dad and ask him for forgiveness for my behavior as a teenager. It was a sunny Wednesday morning. I was nervous. I thought back to a time three decades earlier when I was in my early twenties and drove a six-hour drive from Chicago to Southern Illinois to visit Dad. It didn't have a good outcome. Now thirty years later, I was going to see Dad for a different reason. I was aware that Dad's response to me could be just as unpredictable as it was in the past, but the difference now was that I wasn't going in my own strength, I was no longer intimidated, I wasn't trying to find answers from Dad anymore. God had asked me to do this.

At 57 years old, I nervously knocked on the door, and Dad invited me in. He was alone; his wife was playing cards with friends. I was surprised at how comfortable I felt with him. I only saw Dad at weddings, funerals, and holidays at my sister's. He was older now, even a little feeble. He offered me something to drink, and I watched him as he chose a glass, filled it with ice and water. He placed a napkin on the coffee table and set the glass carefully on it. He was meticulous, and I realized that there so much about Dad that I didn't know.

The two couches in the living room were positioned like an L. Dad sat on one side, and I sat on the other.

Dad spoke first, "Was there something you needed, Mimi?" He was tender and loving.

"Yes, Dad, I came to talk about something that God has put on my heart."

Dad looked visibly uncomfortable, and I realized that he thought I came to discuss the abuse.

I felt like I was five again and was surprised when I called him Daddy, "Daddy, when I was young, a teenager, I was very rebellious toward you. And I came to ask you to forgive me."

Dad looked stunned, obviously moved. "No, no, no, Sweetheart. We don't have to go there," Dad said, obviously feeling uncomfortable.

I explained my teenage behavior to him, "Dad, I told you I hated you. I lied to you. I disrespected you, and I dishonored you." Unexpectedly, I dropped to my knees and said, "Daddy, I need to know that you have forgiven me. God sent me to ask you for forgiveness."

For the first time since I was eight years old, Dad bent over and held me and said, "Sissy, I have always loved you. I never meant to hurt you, ever. I remember the day you were born, holding you in my arms and being in awe of how precious you were. I remember watching you grow. You were always beautiful to me, and I will always love you." *Dad was blessing me.*

"I forgive you, Mimi. But it's me that needs to ask you for forgiveness."

I looked up and saw the tears in his eyes, "I forgive you, Daddy. I forgive you. I love you."

After a long moment, we were both aware of the close affection we had demonstrated toward each other. Even though it had been decades since my Dad held me, it felt so natural. I took my place on the couch, and Dad sat next to me. We talked about the kids and caught up on years of life. It was the beginning, a new beginning, and he laughed as I shared about the adorable antics of my three beautiful children. I noticed that instead of sitting across from me, he was sitting next to me, close to me. It was unusual even for what we had just experienced. It wasn't intimidating; it wasn't wrong, just different. And I would discover why years later.

146

HE HEARS OUR PRAYERS

During Dad's last days on this earth, another mystery leading to more redemption would be revealed. Dad was not well. Years of smoking, drinking, working and being exposed to asbestos at the steel mill caused a tremendous toll on his body. Throughout the years, he battled a stroke, heart attack, and cancer.

A few months after my visit with Dad, his wife called me, "Mimi, Dad's in the hospital. It doesn't look good. I think you need to go see him."

I could hear the urgency in her voice as she explained that Dad was in ICU. Tom was out of town, and I couldn't get a sitter until that evening. I was angry and anxious, fearing I would miss my opportunity to say good-bye to Dad. By the time I could get to the hospital, it was very late, and Dad was alone. Even though it was after hours, they let me in. I was surprised at how fragile Dad looked as I walked in the room and saw him supported by machines, wires, and tubes. His face was contorted, and he looked like he was in pain. I took his hand.

I prayed, "Have mercy on Dad, Lord. Have mercy. He's suffering. I believe he's trying, Lord. Please help him."

Dad moaned an eerie moan; he was obviously battling. I prayed fervently.

I assumed it was acute pain when he woke up startled. "Mimi! Mimi!"

"Yes, Dad, it's me," I answered.

Dad's heart rate was high, and even though the nurses came in, he wouldn't let go of my hand. When his heart rate settled and the nurses left the room, Dad shared with me what he had experienced.

"I was in the dark. A dark being was pulling me down. Horrific. I wasn't strong enough to pull away, and I couldn't escape him. A demon kept pulling me down deeper and deeper, and I thought, 'I'm dying, and I am going to hell.' I have never felt so scared. And then an angel, with a sword, cut him away from me. The angel took me by the hand and brought me back to the surface. When I woke up, I saw you holding my hand. You're God's Angel."

I bent over and held him, wires and all, so relieved he was OK and said, "Daddy, I'm no angel. God sent me here to pray for you. He sent the angel to rescue you from the enemy. But let's agree that from now on, you and I will pray together."

Dad agreed, "Yes, Sissy. From now on." Dad recovered from that hospital visit, but hospital visits became the norm for Dad throughout the remainder of his life. I attempted to call Dad more frequently, and before we hung up, we always prayed together.

WONDERFUL WEDNESDAYS

Elsie became a family friend. She came to our house many Friday nights and to play games like Yahtzee, Chameleon, and Dominoes. Elsie loved games, and she was sharp as a tack and still very competitive. As you can imagine, simply getting dressed was a challenge for Elsie. Opening jars were close to impossible for her. Tom and I agreed that I would spend every Wednesday helping her any way she needed. I took her laundry to her daughters, drove her to the bank, opened her jars of food, and poured them into easy-to-open Tupperware containers. She loved Panera's Harvest Squash Soup. So, during the Fall, I picked up her favorite soup, and we would do lunch in her small apartment and talk about what had transpired in each other's lives since the last time we were together.

Elsie's purpose was to pray and help people walk in the freedom Jesus purchased for them. I became an intercessory partner with her as she prayed with people. I saw miracles happen while I sat

148

next to her in her little apartment. People of every size, color, denomination, and economic status would come to her tiny apartment with hopes of encountering Jesus by praying with an 80-year-old woman. She treated everyone the same. No condemnation.

Men shared how they were abused as little boys and about their sexuality. She would lead them to God the way she led me to Him years ago, and they would encounter Jesus and walk away free. Women would come reeling with pain from marital abuse. She would lead them to God, and they would walk away with hope. Each time it was unique, and each time the person left feeling loved, valued, prized, and accepted. God works in mysterious ways.

I had heard someone adamantly say that people who abuse children have an incurable disease.

So, one Wednesday, I asked Elsie, "Does God save people who abuse children, or as the world says, do they have an incurable disease?"

I went on with questions, "How can a person who violates children be forgiven? How is it possible?"

Elsie asked me, "What punishment do you think would adequately fit the crime?"

"I really don't know," I answered.

"Do you think stripping him naked in public would reciprocate the humiliation he caused you?" she asked.

I thought about it, "Yes," I answered.

"What if he were beaten or whipped for the pain he caused?" she asked.

149

"It's a little harsh, but I think that would be fair," I answered.

"What if he was exposed in a public square naked for all to spit on, sneer and degrade him for what he has done?"

"That's really severe, but I think people who violate children probably deserve it.

I was surprised at her response, "I do too."

Then she asked, "What do you think would be the proper punishment for the things you have done?"

Terror struck my heart. "I don't know. I can't bear to think of it," I answered.

"I understand," she said. "God is the only person who has the wisdom to judge. He alone knows the condition of a human heart."

"The truth is some people who abuse children are stuck in a pattern that they don't understand. They want out and struggle immensely. While others are evil to the core, they will continue to justify their actions and do not want to stop; they often want to capitalize on their actions and exploit others for their benefit."

"When Jesus was stripped, beaten, whipped, mercilessly nailed to a tree naked in public, hanging in agony, struggling for every breath, writhing in pain, watching on-lookers sneer at Him, spit on Him, and speak degrading comments to Him, He was taking your father's place."

"In fact, He took the place of anyone who has ever lived and who will ever live. He paid everyone's debt so that everyone's sins could be removed. His desire is for all of us to come to Him to be forgiven and have our hearts cleansed from evil."

"If we reject what He purchased for us, we reject the truth that His love has the power to save us and redeem sin. If we accept Him and what He accomplished, we receive freedom from sin's power over us. If your father is searching for God and wants to be cleansed from unrighteousness, He will find it in Jesus. Jesus purchased your father with His blood and buried your father's sins with him in the grave. Through Him, all sins are forgiven."

"Elsie, God has revealed his forgiveness to me so many times. Why do I get stuck in unbelief sometimes?" I asked, exasperated with myself.

"Mary Ann, God is the perfect one. Not us. The experiences we have when we are younger have a profound influence on us. They shape us and our perspectives. God knows that and is patient. He is patient in the process. Keep returning to Him. Keep seeking Him. He is not upset with you. He loves you."

"It seems like a toggle back and forth," I explained to Elsie.

"At some point in time, you have to draw a line in the sand or plunge a stake in the ground and say, 'truth is truth' and stick with it. You will get there, and He will help you," she said confidently.

DAD TALKS TO JESUS

Dad's wife called! Dad was in the hospital!! It was serious!!!

"I'm afraid he's not coming home, Mimi. You may want to get over there and see him," I could feel the urgency in her voice.

I told Tom, and he said, "Go over there, and be your father's advocate."

Fearful, I answered, "His advocate? I don't know how to do that."

Tom responded, "You'll know what to do when you get there. Stay as long as you need."

The drive to the hospital in Illinois was approximately one hour. I prayed the entire way. When I arrived in Dad's room, I was shocked. Dad looked so fragile and frail. His wife was sitting next to his bed, exhausted. She was very dedicated to Dad, and she needed to go home and get rest.

"I have his underwear and his pants with me," she said as she patted her canvas bag.

"OK?" I spoke with a questioning look on my face.

"He's tried to break out of here several times, and we can't let him do that. He won't survive if he does. He can't leave this room without clothes. If he gets up looking for pants, tell him I took them home with me."

"Oh, my goodness, are you serious?" I asked.

"Totally." We both chuckled, and I took her place in the chair next to his bed.

Dad had throat cancer and was being fed directly into his stomach. He looked like a bag of bones. The next couple of days were grueling as I watched Dad suffer. I sat on his bed and held his hand while he slept. Several doctors and nurses were managing his care. I remembered that Tom told me to be his advocate, so I took notes when they came in and asked them to spell words I didn't understand. When Dad's wife wasn't there, I reported to her what they said. The staff got their wires crossed numerous times, and I had to clarify to one doctor how the other was treating Dad. Tom was 100% correct. Dad needed an advocate, and his wife couldn't be there 24 hours a day.

Nurse after nurse tried their best to feed him and medicate Dad intravenously, but his veins kept collapsing.

He finally looked at me and cried and said, "Get me out of here, Mimi."

I knew only one place to go, and while nurses were doing their best to care for him, I went to the corner and cried out to the Lord. "Father, I can't handle watching Dad be poked with needle after needle. It's inhumane! There has to be some other way."

And God directed me, "Ask him if he is angry?"

"OK, but please help me," I felt desperate.

After the nurses left, I sat next to Dad and held his hand. He kept drifting in and out of sleep, and every time he woke up, he looked surprised to see me.

"Mimi, what are you doing here?" he asked.

"Spending time with you, Dad," I repeated.

"Why would you want to do that?" he asked.

"Because I love you, Dad," I answered every time.

Then I asked Dad, "Dad, can I ask you a question?"

"Sure, Sweetie, what do you want to know?"

"Are you angry?"

"Why, no, honey. I'm not angry."

I took a deep breath. "Dad, God told me that you were angry. And he asked me to ask you about it." There was a silent pause.

"I don't know what to say," Dad said, sounding puzzled.

So, I asked, "Would you be willing to pray with me about it?"

"Sure," he replied hesitantly.

"Do you want to pray first, or do you want me to pray?" I asked.

"Why don't you pray," he replied.

"OK," I replied. "God, I thank you for Dad, I thank you for his life, and I thank you that you love him, and you are with us here, right now. I thought I heard you say that Dad was angry, and you wanted me to ask him about it. Dad isn't sure, and that is why we are praying—to ask you for insight and understanding. Would you help us understand why you wanted me to ask Dad if he was angry?"

Dad squeezed my hand. "Dad, did God reveal anything to you?"

"Yes," he replied weakly.

"What did God say to you?" I asked.

"I am angry," Dad answered. "I am angry … at myself."

"Do you want to talk about it?" I asked.

"There really isn't a lot to talk about. I am angry about how I mistreated people, your mother, my children, and others."

"Would you be willing to take that anger to God, Dad?" I gently asked.

"Yes," Dad answered tiredly.

"OK, why don't you pray this time," I added.

Dad was thoughtful and prayed, "Father, I sinned against you, my children, their mother, and so many other people. I don't have a right to come to you, and I don't deserve to be forgiven..."

Dad's prayer went on for a little while when I interrupted him, "Dad, why don't we take one thing at a time. Let's start with how you mistreated your family. Why don't you confess that?"

"Father, I mistreated my children and the mother of my children. Would you please forgive me?"

And then Dad began to go the next issue.

I interrupted Dad again, "Dad, if you ask someone a question, do you think you should honor them by waiting for their response?"

"Yes, of course, I do," he answered a little indignantly.

"Well, you just asked God if he forgave you. Don't you think you should wait to hear his response?"

"Well, yes. I should," he answered.

"Why don't you ask him again." Dad did, he asked God to forgive him, and he silently bowed his head and listened. I saw a tear drop, and he squeezed my hand.

"What did he say, Dad?"

"He said 'Forgiven,'" Dad whispered.

"Let's thank him, Dad." And Dad prayed a prayer of thanksgiving.

"What else do you want to bring to him, Dad?" Dad brought a series of trespasses that he had harbored. Sins against his children, against others, and at last, God revealed to Dad that he was carrying a sin of self-hatred. Dad said that he could never forgive himself for all that he had done and that he didn't deserve life in Heaven. He was afraid to die because he should go to hell, and he knew there was nothing he could do to earn his way to Heaven.

"Dad, it's not our decision who goes to hell or who goes to Heaven."

So, we brought that to Jesus too, and we waited to hear God's reply. "What did he say to you, Dad?"

"I just keep hearing, 'Forgiven.' How could that be?"

"Dad, I have faced the same questions. None of us feel worthy of being forgiven. God's love is more powerful than our weakness. What He accomplished on the cross is more powerful than our sins. Do you think you might want to thank him?" I asked.

Dad laughed a weak laugh, "Yes. Thank you, Father. Thank you, Jesus."

"Dad, can we ask God a couple more questions?"

"Yes," Dad answered faintly.

"God, would you tell Dad if you are able to redeem the mistakes Dad made and the sins that Dad committed?" Dad squeezed my hand tight as he heard from the Lord.

"What did he say?" I asked Dad,

"He said 'Ask Me'," Dad responded.

Dad asked, "Father, please redeem the many sins I have committed. Please don't hold my sins against my children. Please help them to know you," Dad's eyes were filled with tears.

I added to Dad's prayer, "God, you heard Dad's cry. Would you please respond to Dad?"

Dad looked at me incredulously and repeated what he heard God say, "It's done."

We smiled at each other. "It's Jesus, Dad. He can do anything," we smiled again.

I felt the sacredness of the moment.

"Yes, He can," Dad agreed.

"I know you're tired, and nurses will be here soon. Can we ask God one more question?"

"Yes, what's that?" Now I knew why God had revealed Dad's identity to me during that first time Elsie prayed with me many years ago. The time that Jesus pinned the demon to the wall and declared that Dad was His son.

I asked, "Jesus, who is Dad to you?" I held Dad's hand and waited for God to reveal to Dad his true identity. Dad looked like he was in anguish. We waited, and Jesus spoke to Dad.

And Dad whispered the answer without me asking, "I'm his son." Dad's countenance changed. He looked radiant.

"That's what I heard too, Dad." He couldn't get up to hug me because he was so weak, and there were many wires about him, so I found a place where I could lay down next to him, and we rested feeling the peace of God's presence surround us.

While I laid next to Dad, and before he fell asleep, he shared something with me.

"Mimi, do you remember when you came to visit me years ago, and you asked me to forgive you?"

"Yes, Dad," I answered.

"Well, that morning, before you came, I had gotten down on my knees, and I asked God if He would show me what repentance looks like. And just hours later, you knocked on my door. I couldn't believe my ears," Dad shared.

I reflected back to that morning. *That's why Dad looked so stunned when I confessed my teenage behavior and asked him to forgive me.*

"That must have taken a lot of courage to do," Dad added.

"It was a blessing, Dad," I answered, "it was by God's design."

"Yes, it was, Sweetie."

Dad recovered and was home within days. Weak and fragile, but home. And Sandy cared for him faithfully until the next time.

WHY AM I STILL HERE?

We all knew that Dad wasn't going to be with us for much longer. My brother came home from New Jersey to spend time with Dad. One morning during my brother's visit at Dad's, Tom woke me up early. "Mary Ann, watch this video! Watch it and take it to your Dad. He needs to see this."

I sat up in bed and watched the 18-minute video. "Wow, Dad keeps asking me, "Mimi, why am I still here? Why doesn't God just take me? I think this is the reason."

I used to tease Dad every time he asked me that question, "Mimi, I just can't understand why I'm still here," and I would answer, "Dad, we're all scratching our heads about that one," and he would laugh in response.

Tom interrupted my memory, "Mary Ann, you need to take this to your Dad right now."

"Right now? It's 6:00 a.m.?" I resisted.

"I know, but I feel an urgency. You need to go now," he urged insistently.

As you have probably already discerned from the many stories I have shared with you that Tom is very sensitive to the leading of the Holy Spirit, and God has led him in so many ways to guide and protect me. I felt uncomfortable taking that video to Dad in this way, but after 20 years of marriage, I knew that if Tom felt it was that important, I should just follow his lead.

On the way to Dad's, I began to panic. It was probably just warfare, but I began telling God that I just didn't feel comfortable bringing a video to Dad and telling him he should watch it. It just seemed kind of critical or disrespectful for some reason. While driving East on Interstate 270, approaching the 367 exit to Illinois, the heavens opened up before me. I saw Heaven. It was glorious. Jesus was on a magnificent throne, and a man was standing next to Him. I knew that man was my grandfather, my Dad's Dad. Grandpa Huber, who died when I was five, spoke to me from Heaven.

He said, "Tell your Dad to finish what I didn't," and the vision disappeared.

I grasped the reality that I wasn't intruding, and I wasn't 'parenting' Dad. The video was an Ancient Path that would answer the prayers he prayed in the hospital about his children's welfare, their identity, and their destiny. The video is called "Imparting a Father's Blessing," created by Craig Hill. In it, he describes the value and the importance of a father speaking blessing over his children.

Here we go.

Fortunately, everyone was up drinking coffee when I reached Dad's house at 7:30 a.m. Both of my brothers were sitting at the kitchen table when I walked into the house through the sliding glass door that led to the kitchen from the carport.

"Mimi, what are you doing here?" Dad asked.

"Dad, you have been asking us for some time, 'Why am I still here?' I think I know why. Tom woke me up early this morning and asked me to share this video with you, and I think it holds some answers."

Dad respected Tom and was very open to watching the video.

We went back to the sitting room, and Dad sat in his Lazy-Boy. I knelt next to him as I sat my laptop on his lap and hit the play button. Dad watched the video intently. I could tell the video moved him.

I wasn't sure of his reaction, so when it concluded, I explained, "Dad, I felt uncomfortable about bringing this video to you. I was complaining to myself on the way, and I know this sounds way out there and a little crazy, but on the way here, the heavens opened up, and I saw Grandpa Huber. He was standing next to Jesus' throne, and he told me to tell you, 'Finish what I didn't.' You may think I am nuts, but ..."

Dad interrupted me, saying, "Mimi, I don't think you're crazy. Do you remember that day when you came to me and asked me to forgive you?"

160

"Yes, Dad, I remember," I answered.

"When I held you, and we cried?"

"Yes, Dad.

"I could smell my Dad. I even sat close to you on the couch because I could smell my Dad, and I couldn't get close enough to him. I loved my Dad, and I respected my Dad. I wanted to please my Dad. And I think God was preparing me then for what you are showing me now."

That's why he sat so close to me on the couch that morning.

Before I left, Dad blessed both of my brothers, and he blessed me, "Mimi, you are my daughter. You are a strong woman of faith, and I'm proud of you and the woman you have become. I love you."

Tears.

A week later, one of my sisters called to tell me that Dad called and told her that she was beautiful.

God works in mysterious ways.

SHE WHISPERED, "I AM BEAUTIFUL"

Tom and I agreed that since the kids were approaching the age where they would be graduating high school, I needed to prepare for returning to the marketplace and was eager to learn. Since coaching and training have always been important to me, I became certified in several leadership and training programs.

Tommy was attending College in Kentucky. Johnny and Iris were still being homeschooled. Johnny was a strong swimmer and wanted to compete on a State Level. Since Johnny was homeschooled, he was ineligible to compete at the state level. To be eligible, Johnny needed to be enrolled in a public or private school. Thus, he began attending a local Christian High School and joined their swim team. Each parent was asked to volunteer 20 hours of service to the school. I approached the Superintendent and discussed various leadership programs I could offer the school. He asked me to meet with Terri, the school's guidance counselor, to best understand their students' needs.

Terri is a phenomenal person. Her heart was to equip these kids for life. When I asked her about areas that were most important for the Middle and High School students, she responded, "That they would know their true value and identity. They don't need adults to come in and tell them what they should do. They need adults to be authentic and transparent. They need real stories of transformation and hope."

I felt the nudge in my heart to share my story with her. Terri listened intently as I shared details. When I was done, she asked, "would you be willing to share this with the girls in this school?"

I hesitated before I said yes, "Terri, Johnny doesn't know this part of my life. In fact, none of my children do. I don't want to embarrass him. Can you give me a couple of days to talk with him and get his blessing?"

"Yes, of course," she responded.

That afternoon, I picked up Johnny from school, and as we pulled into the driveway of our home. I asked Johnny if we could sit in the van for a moment, and I shared the details of my life BC (Before Christ). When I was finished sharing my story with my 16-year-old son, I asked, "I have been talking with Miss Terri, and she and I believe my story may help some of the girls in your school. Before I do that, I want to be sure that you are OK with this. If it causes you any embarrassment, I will refrain from sharing.

Johnny looked up at me and said, "Mom, if you can help one girl in that school by sharing your story, you have to do it."

I was so proud of him. I called Terri the next day, and we began planning how to best start.

I met with each of the Bible Study teachers ahead of time and exchanged ideas. One of the teachers told me that each year she administers an anonymous survey to ask the girls to honestly share how they feel about themselves. I was shocked as I read the responses specifically to the question, "How do I feel about myself?" Here is a sample of the survey results:

Ugly
Insignificant
I'll always fail
No one likes me
No guy will ever like me for me
I am a bad person
I am a burden
Undesirable
I have no talent
I have no purpose
I'm a slut
I'm not a slut, but people think I am
I will never be good enough
I'm a mess
I will never be attractive to a man
I am unlovable
People don't truly like me
No one cares
I don't belong
I wish I were taller
I wish I were shorter
I wish I were thinner
I wish I were friendlier
I wish I were quieter
I wish I were a different color
I wish I were more fun
I am going to end up alone
I will never have enough money
I will never recover from my loss
I can't keep up
I will never please my parents
I will never please my teachers
I will never please my friends
I am not important
I am stupid
I don't deserve to be happy

I looked up at her and asked for the positive list. She looked at me solemnly and said, "there is none." *Oh, my goodness.*

"I need to pray about this. Can I get back with you about some ideas on how to address these lies?" I asked.

We agreed to meet the following week. My respect for her grew as I witnessed her love for these girls. She sincerely and genuinely cared. It's no wonder most of her students called her "Mom."

After my encounter with Jesus, when He dressed me in a beautiful white robe, crowned my head, placed a ring on my finger and beautiful sandals on my feet, I began working on a document that affirmed my true identity. (You can find that document on my website, lovetriumphs.com, as a free downloadable pdf). I sat in my bedroom, looking at the list from the survey and comparing it to my list; I began to cry. I remembered feeling those feelings of ugliness, fear, self-hatred, awkwardness, angst. I know how often they try to creep back into my being. "Oh, dear God, they don't know who they are. Can they have the same breakthrough you gave me?"

Here is a sample of my list:

I am known.	I am never without help
I am lovable.	I am a priority
I am chosen.	I am accepted
I am valuable	I am rescued
I am cherished	I am forgiven
I am accepted	I am redeemed
I am highly regarded	I am whole
I am distinctly crafted	I am innocent
I am uniquely made	I am safe
I am significant	I am set apart
I am beautiful	I am prized
I am significant	I am beautiful
I have purpose	I am healed
I have a calling	I am free
I am never alone	I am protected

They all knew that they had taken the survey, but they had not seen each other's answers. Each young lady was not aware that they were not the only one who lacked confidence, self-esteem, or self-worth. It became clear to me what we needed to do together.

I listed all of their answers on one page without names, and to protect each person from embarrassment, I asked each young lady to stand up and read one statement that was not hers. Each of these beautiful and promising young ladies stood up from her desk and declared what they collectively felt:

"I am ugly."

"I am insignificant."

"I don't measure up."

"No one likes me."

"I am a slut."

Hearing the lies that had been planted in each heart was more powerful than just reading them. While listening, my stomach felt like someone punched it with a fierce blow. I hurt for them. After they had each stood up and read, the room was silent. Some had tears in their eyes. Many looked down at their desks incredulously. It was evident that they had all believed damaging lies. What now?

We talked about Satan's strategy to distort the truth about who we are, as well as who God is. We discussed the true nature of Jesus. He is love, and all that He does is for good. He was not behind these destructive descriptors. It was time to face the truth and receive our true identity.

I asked them to close their eyes, and we asked Jesus to speak into each heart and share with them the first time they believed that lie and write it down. Each of them was writing. God was in the room. You could hear silent sobs and sniffles. Jesus was speaking to them.

Thank you, Jesus!

165

Then I passed out my list. It was made up of three columns: (1) What the Father says about me, (2) What Jesus says and me, and (3) What the Holy Spirit says about me. I asked them to take a minute and read each 'I am' statement silently. What would be different about reading this time, is that God was going to tell them who they are by highlighting one of the truths about their identity from the page. We prayed, and I asked God to reveal to each of them which truth He was speaking over them at that moment.

"Don't overthink it. It will bounce off the page to you. Highlight, underline, or circle it quickly." I added.

Once they did that, I then asked each of these young ladies to stand up and share the statement God was speaking over them.

The first girl that shared was tall, attractively dressed with not a hair out of place. One would think she would stand up and say, "I am valuable," but she stood up with tears in her eyes and bravely claimed, "I am forgiven."

The second young lady was heavier, short, curly black hair, big blue eyes, and stated, "I have purpose."

The third was medium height, slender build, straight black hair, deep brown eyes, of Asian descent; she stood up and said, "I am free."

The fourth had dark skin, dark eyes, her hair was braided, she had an athletic build, and she stood up and stated, "I am rescued."

Sharing these positive truths about their identity went on, row after row, with each young lady claiming their identity from God until the middle row. We will call her Belinda (not her real name). I couldn't see her eyes because her hair covered them as she looked down at her desk.

I reached out by asking, "Belinda, what has God highlighted for you?"

She was silent.

I gently prodded, "Belinda, I know that He highlighted something very important and significant that is meant just for you; what is it, sweetheart?"

She stayed silent.

I knelt by her desk and brushed back her hair. She was crying. Belinda was abused by her Dad, left by her mom. She was alone in the world. Her life was hard, and she looked for other boys to give her significance which had created more rejection and abuse. As tenderly as I could, I spoke to her, "Belinda, he leaves the ninety-nine to rescue the one. You are the one. You are His one. What has he highlighted?"

She whispered, and I couldn't hear her.

"I'm sorry. I didn't hear you. Would you repeat it a little louder?

She whispered a little louder, "I am beautiful."

Tears were streaming down all of our eyes.

"Yes. That is the truth. You are beautiful. Would you stand and state that the same way He spoke it over you?"

Belinda stood and stated with a renewed confidence, "I am beautiful."

Some of the young ladies got up from their desks to hug her and affirm, "yes, you are beautiful." She cried for a little while, and everyone returned to their desks. After each of them stood up and made their statement, we closed by writing to God a letter thanking Him for the truth.

The next day, during the morning assembly, wonderful worship was filling the auditorium, and I looked over at Belinda. She was wearing a dress and makeup. Her hair was clean, combed, and curled. Her lips were adorned with lipstick, her eyes were dry now, and her hands were raised high as she praised the God who makes all things new.

She has a road ahead of her, Lord; please cover her and help her stay close to the truth.

I felt a whisper, "I will," from the Lord.

Those young ladies fueled the passion within me to write my story. I realized that I had been just like them – thinking lies and believing I was the only one. I knew then that my purpose would be to reveal the true nature of Jesus so he can reveal His children's true identity. I was never the same after that season.

How, Lord? How do I find my place to serve You? I want to be Your ambassador. I want to be Your herald. I want to be Your emissary!

SAYING GOODBYE TO DAD AND ELSIE

Dad was in and out of the hospital many times, but he entered for the last time. I walked into his room, and he was alone. I sat next to him and held his hand. I knew this was it.

He didn't look up, but he spoke to me, "Mimi?"

"Yes, Dad," I whispered.

By name, Dad began to bless his family. He started with his wife and proceeded to bless my siblings.

168

"Sandy has been a good wife."

I echoed, "Yes, she is the best Dad."

"I don't know how she puts up with me; he replied."

I smiled to myself in agreement, "She loves you, Dad. We all love you."

He proceeded, "Matt is faithful. He is a good man."

"Yes, he is, Dad."

"And Suzanne, she was always my princess."

I thought back decades ago when we were young, and Dad always called her his princess, and I smiled. "She always has been, Dad."

"And John is a fine young man. I'm so proud of him."

"He is, Dad, very fine."

"And Nancy, she could always make me laugh and smile."

"You and everyone else, Dad," I answered in agreement.

"And Cassy is so helpful and loyal."

"It's true, Dad; she is very precious."

"Lisa is a good woman." "Yes, she is, Dad."

He blessed his wife and all of his children—another sacred moment.

His room was filled with family, and he died in the middle of the night. When Dad left this earth, those of us around his bed felt him leave the room. And we were grateful he was in pain no longer.

I wrote this parable in honor of Dad's life. It's a compilation of the Gospel as well as Matthew 8:22 and Matthew 13:44

The Pearl of Great Price

There once was a kindhearted and diligent laborer. While he was laboring in the field, he found a hidden treasure. He looked at the treasure thoughtfully. Even though it was covered in grime, plaque, and gravel, he was certain that a special solvent he owned would restore it completely. He wanted to possess it, so he hid it again. As he finished his day, he smiled confidently to himself. Enthusiastically, he went home and sold all his possessions to purchase the field and obtain the treasure.

The next day, the laborer bought the field. He was mocked and made fun of, "How foolish he is to sell all that he owned to purchase a field that will only cause him trouble!" But his mind was set. Their jeering remarks did not move him. His heart was fixed on gaining the treasure. Upon receiving the deed to the field, he was filled with joy and eagerly went to the place where he hid the treasure the day before.

As the laborer dug out his treasure, he beamed with delight. He held it close to him as he brought it into his father's house. His hands carefully and gently wiped away the grime, the plaque, and the gravel. The treasure gleamed brilliantly back at him. The laborer gave it a special place of honor in his father's home, where it was forever cherished.

Who is this laborer? What is this treasure? Why did the laborer sell all he had to possess it?

The laborer is Jesus. The treasure is Dad, and you, and me. The field is the world. The grime, the plaque, and the gravel are the cares and worries, the iniquities and offenses, and the disappointments and pain we carry from being in the world. The property that Jesus willingly sold to obtain the treasure is His

170

very life. The special solvent is His blood. And the house is God's Kingdom. The reason? He cherishes us. It was in His Father's heart from the foundation of time to seek and rescue us from this world, and it is with gladness and joy He joins us to Himself.

Dad was a pearl of great price that Jesus came to rescue, restore and bring into His Father's Kingdom.

Three mornings later, I woke up earlier than usual. As I began to sit up in my bed, the most remarkable thing happened, Dad appeared to me. I never believed that anything like that could really happen. But it did. I just saw his face. He looked a lot younger, in his 30s. He was beaming, glowing. He was at rest, at peace. He was childlike and full of joy. And although he didn't talk to me, his eyes spoke to me.

He was fully present, and his eyes were clear and blue as he spoke, "Mimi, if you could only see what I see. If you could only see what is in store for you."

Instantly, I felt excited to experience the City not made by mere human hands, but by a miraculous God. Like being on the other end of the phone with someone who is on a glorious holiday at the beach, I sensed that Heaven will be a glorious dwelling place.

I spontaneously responded by exclaiming, "Dad! You made it!"

Tears filled my eyes, he acknowledged my excitement with a smile, and he was gone. The room was silent. I felt the weight of the moment, got down on my knees, and prayed, "Thank you, Father, for this gracious gift. For letting me know that Dad is OK. Dad is with you."

Shortly after Dad's death, our family moved from St. Louis, Missouri, to Atlanta, Georgia, in February of 2016. Elsie's health was deteriorating. I returned to Missouri to visit her that Summer and be with her for the last time. She was feeble and as amazing as always. When the nursing home staff members came into her room, they told me how miraculously she touched the lives around her. She never stopped introducing people to Jesus. Before I left, Elsie blessed me and encouraged me to be fearless and brave and tell my story. Elsie died and went to be with Jesus on December 22, 2016. I can only imagine how much Heaven loved receiving her.

SILVER LININGS

I struggled with writing this story. Where do I begin. What parts should I share? How do I share them? I would go to a quiet place in the morning and by noon bring to Tom what I had written. He would read it and, fortunately, tell me the truth, "Mary Ann, it's a little too preachy" or "I'm sorry, Sweetheart, it's too flat." So, I went to the House of Prayer in Atlanta to sit before the Lord and ask Him, "Jesus, would you give me this book, or would you take it away." And He answered by saying, "You need intercession."

Of course.

At 11:00 a.m. that day, I went home and private messaged every woman who was familiar with my story and asked that they pray for me. Within the hour I got messages from them saying they were praying.

The next thing I knew, Iris knocked at the door, "Mom, dinner's ready."

Surprised I responded, "Dinner? What happened to lunch time?"

Iris answered, "Mom, it's 5:30."

I had been writing for over five hours and didn't realize it.

Iris looked over what I wrote and suggested, "As a reader, it would be really important to know what you were feeling as you experienced the things you did. Why don't share what you were feeling and thinking in italics." And my story came to life.

Sarah, my daughter-in-law, an English major, read it and helped me understand that I was writing my story as a sequence events, but my story is more like a circle of redemption. She helped me share my story with depth and meaning.

I found that listening to worship, soaking in it, allowing all my own ideas and thoughts to be suspended, and be still before the Lord, gave room to hearing Jesus to speak to me about my story. He helped me remember what I experienced, how I was feeling, and gave me perspective I didn't have as a young person.

In 2017, I was still writing my book and my consulting business expanded to Upstate New York. Each month I travelled to Rochester, NY for one week to call on corporate clients for a major leadership training company. My business steadily grew, but in March 2020, the World Health Organization declared COVID-19 a pandemic. The Center for Disease Control and Prevention issued recommended workplace guidelines, and everyone's life was turned upside down. Most businesses were required to social distance by instituting policies where people worked remotely from home, and my professional life came to a screeching halt.

For three years, I worked relentlessly developing key corporate relationships in Upstate New York to train employees in leadership, team building, and communication. All our training was delivered in person, which was no longer considered safe. We quickly adapted to online platforms, but my season serving in New York was coming to an end. It was a huge loss of income for me, and I was so very disappointed. But there was a bigger silver lining.

I began to host a ZOOM Prayer Room in the early morning hours before work started and another at noon, during lunch break. The ZOOM Prayer Rooms grew from two to four within a matter of months. Amid an isolated world, the ZOOM Prayer Rooms became sacred places where women met to cast all their cares upon the Lord, and He met us *every time*. We read God's word, then we prayed, and then we listened. And He spoke to us, *every time*. He comforted us with His Presence, He led us during uncertainty, He healed us from fear and past wounds. And the He is continuing to minister to us today.

It is often said that when you fall, God picks you up, dusts you off, and puts you back in the game. That's a worldly perspective of God. The truth is that when a person falls, Jesus bends down and brushes the hair from their eyes. He looks past the shame, guilt, and remorse, and into their eyes to reveal His love. He tenderly wipes their tears away and kindly quiets the fear. If we have done something wrong, He imparts wisdom so the mistake will not be repeated. If something has been done wrong to us, He gives insight so we can forgive. He crowds out the lies with loving truth so that we can walk in fellowship with Him. He extends His hand, lifts us up, puts His arm around us, and with a knowing smile, says, "Let's do it together this time."

Life was never meant to do alone. No matter what you have experienced, seek God with all your heart, His love will triumph over every trouble.

###

Come Join Us

You have read my story. Like millions of people, I was a normal kid who lived a normal life and then found myself being sexually abused by adults and peers I should have been able to trust. My story is unique because I have experienced so much healing and redemption through encounters with God.

I know you have a story, too. And your story is important. Your voice is important. Even though I have not met you, I know this about you: You are valuable. You are uniquely made and distinctly crafted. You have been given gifts, and you have a calling. Your life is significant. You are a priority to God. You are set apart and appreciated for who you are. Your story matters because you matter.

God is talking to you. Hearing Him is important because He has so much to tell you. Recognizing His voice is important because there are so many messages pouring into our minds. He does not expect you to figure everything out. He wants to guide you along your unique journey with Him. He wants to comfort you, heal you, protect you, and provide for you.

Reading my story may have stirred emotions about your own story. Perhaps you have a desire to know God more intimately. I invite you pray this prayer with me.

"Father, I want to know a God who is so kind He swings with children and makes them laugh. I want to know a God whose tender touch can quiet the storms of life. I want to know a God who is not ashamed of me in my weakness but is committed to me as a daughter/son. I want to know a God who is so powerful, He pins demons to the wall. I want to know a God who loves me, no matter what I have done or what has been done to me. I want to know You. I invite you into every part of my life. Please help me know You as You really are. Please help me overcome the lies I believe about myself and know myself as You created me. I am excited about my future with you. In Jesus Name. Amen."

I invite you to visit my website and join a community of women who are growing together and closer to God. Seeking God and hearing His voice will bring you peace as He gives you clarity about unresolved issues, your identity, and your purpose.

Thank you for reading my story. It has been an honor to share it with you. Please reach out and tell me how it impacted you. If you found it valuable, share it with a friend who needs hope today. Let's stay in touch - visit me at www.lovetriumphs.com.

With Love,

Mary Ann

Hear What Women Say About Love Triumphs!

Love Triumphs! came into my life at a time when I was lonely and confused and feeling let down by the closest people in my life. I discovered friendship and fellowship with mature Christian women and an opportunity to draw nearer to the Lord. I appreciate how Mary Ann opens her heart and offers love, time and dedication to any woman seeking closer relationship with the Lord.

Hala Hannoush - Georgia
Fervent Believer

I joined Love Triumphs! in Spring 2020 shortly after our world shut down due to COVID 19. This weekly time with the Lord and these women, my sisters in Christ, has blessed and expanded not only my prayer life, but my life in general. Our time together was a true lifeline during the months of quarantine and has since become my "safe place". There is no judging, no impatience with each other's stories or needs—only true Godly love as He ministers to us through each other's stories and lives. I have experienced life changing breakthrough in the Prayer Room- freedom from guilt and shame, unconditional love, divine revelation through Holy Spirit intervention. We laugh and cry together, we encourage each other. It would be difficult to choose a time that stands out more that another because the beautiful truth is God ALWAYS shows up! He shows us His love for each of us as His Daughters....He talks to us and answers our prayers.

Kathryn Guthrie - Alabama
Founder Reclaimed

The first time I experienced 'where two or more are gathered, I am in their midst' was during my first Love Triumphs prayer room. When we come together in prayer, I feel God's love and presence with us. I have experienced the love and compassion of Jesus Christ through Mary Ann, the way she ministers through prayers. His Word comes to life in our prayer time. I have studied the Word of God for 27 years and tried to be good and obedient to Him. But because I did not experience His love and compassion, many times they were just words on a page. It took someone who is compassionate and knows the love of the Lord to help His Word come to life for me. Truth without love can be traumatizing. Trying to measure up can leave us feel beat up. But when we encounter God's love, truth is freedom.

Angela Rosson - Georgia
Founder & Head Coach, Boot Camp 360

When I joined the prayer call one Saturday morning, I was experiencing severe nerve pain in my foot as a frustrating side effect of my recent back surgery. I had dealt with the physical, mental, and emotional ramifications of chronic pain for the better part of 17 years. I showed up to the call that day desperate. I had asked the Lord, "If you are a shield around me, why have I gotten hit by so many of the enemy's arrows? Why do I hurt so bad?" Because I was past the point of niceties, I added, "I'm afraid you're going to give me some lame excuse." I couldn't handle a trite Christian saying that made light of my suffering. The Lord's response to me was, "Those arrows weren't aimed at you; they were aimed at me." This changed everything for me. Instead of wondering why he hadn't protected me, I felt honored to share in the fellowship of his suffering. I saw that Jesus had protected me from experiencing the extent of suffering that he went through, and the pain I had experienced connected me to him in a way I had never experienced before. I felt so close to him.

Want to know a cool side benefit of his caring attention to my pain? At the same time, he healed my heart, the nerve pain in my foot also went away. I am blown away by his goodness to me.

Jamie Weichman - Texas
Co-Founder Breathe Life

The prayer room is a sacred space of intimacy with Jesus. He meets us every time as we read His word and present our questions to Him! He answers our questions and pours out His love over us. My favorite time of the week is joining the prayer room with Mary Ann and the sisters in Christ who open their hearts to hear from and receive the loving kindness of our Savior every single time! His presence and goodness fill the room! We always receive encouragement, blessings and healing through His word, His voice, and His love! This is a beautiful and tangible way to nourish your soul!

Tonya Cohen - Georgia
Founder, The Well

Through Love Triumphs, I feel like I have tasted and seen the goodness of God. The weekly zoom calls are a beautiful place where I am confident that I can come to experience his love, grace, and kindness again and again. God seems to direct the right words tenderly and consistently at the right time to my soul. There is a common theme of raw authenticity among the women who come. Where love is, truth feels safe. I feel like I have gotten to know Him better by listening in on His conversations with others. We come, expectant, and He seems to already be there, happy to greet us and remind us of our worth.

Mary Ann is a gift. Her life is a testimony of God's grace and goodness. She brings her past experiences and present relationship with God to every meeting. I have never met anyone like her. The times that she has led me straight into the presence of God are something I will never forget. When my faith is weak, it is thoughts of this space—this place where I can't deny the realness of God and His love for me, that my doubts lose their power. I'm forever grateful for Love Triumphs and the impact it has had on my life.

Rebecca Cerasani - Georgia
Rebecca Cerasani Photography

179

You know how when you talk with God sometimes, you're not sure you're really listening to Him or making it up in your mind? Well, that doesn't happen when we come together. In the Prayer Room, God speaks to us so clearly. He confirms what He is talking to you through what He tells someone else, or sometimes He gives each of us a part of a puzzle that makes sense when all the pieces come together. It's simply amazing!

It's wonderful how He can bring a group of ladies from different States and Countries as one, before Him, and draw us close to His heart to whisper to us the sweetest revelations that bring us identity, guidance, love, peace, and joy, among other things.

I live in a different Country and time zone than most attendants, and even though it means waking up two hours earlier than everybody, it's totally worth it, because the love and fellowship that I've found here are simply unique. I feel like I've known these beautiful ladies for years, and we've never even been in the same room once. If you haven't experienced something like this, join us, or get certified to start a group of your own, and get ready to go to new heights!

Ana Regina Toledo,
Media Correspondent, Guatemala

180